BLYTHSWOOD CARE

Wonderful!

FOREWORD BY LORD MACKAY OF CLASHFERN
EDITED BY IRENE HOWAT

Wonderful!

BLYTHSWOOD PEOPLE SHARE
STORIES OF GOD'S FAITHFULNESS

CHRISTIAN
FOCUS

Copyright © Blythswood Care 2016

paperback ISBN 978-1-78191-773-2
epub ISBN 978-1-78191-891-3
mobi ISBN 978-1-78191-892-0

10 9 8 7 6 5 4 3 2 1

Published in 2016
by
Christian Focus Publications Ltd,
Geanies House, Fearn, Ross-shire,
IV20 1TW, Great Britain.

www.christianfocus.com

Cover design by
Moose77.com

Printed and bound
by
Bell & Bain, Glasgow

CONTENTS

Lord Mackay of Clashfern

Foreword

❖❖❖

When the late Jackie Ross was a student for the ministry in Glasgow he was conscious that there were many people in that great city who never heard the gospel which was declared regularly in church. He resolved to do what he could to bring that precious message to those who did not ever think of coming to hear it. After discussion with a number of like-minded colleagues it was decided that they should publish and distribute gospel tracts.

Since they were located in the neighbourhood of Blythswood Square the group chose the name of the Blythswood Tract Society and set out on a vigorous spreading of gospel literature. To this was added the declaration of the gospel on the streets in the neighbourhood. After a time meetings were arranged open to all when a gospel address was given and questions answered.

As the group spread out over Scotland so these activities spread. The ministry was primarily the declaration of the Scriptures but soon Jackie and his colleagues appreciated that many of those with whom they came in contact had pressing physical needs and that although the ministry of the Lord Jesus was a preaching ministry it also consisted to a large degree in meeting the physical and health needs of the people.

This encouraged the group to see what they could do to meet the similar needs of those with whom they came in contact. Gradually the activities of Blythswood extended to the care of the needs of body and soul which succinctly describes its work today.

Just as the nature of its work extended so did the area in which it operated. Romania was a principal focus of the work for a time but it has now extended to many other parts of the world.

It is now fifty years since Blythswood started and it is fitting to recognise how God has provided for it over that time. This book is part of that recognition. It illustrates how widespread is Blythswood's sphere of labour and also how diverse are the people who have been influenced by it and have played a part in its work.

May these personal stories of faith encourage us to thank God for His provision for Blythswood over the past fifty years, to pray for its continued success into the future and to do what we can to support its work as an outstandingly deserving Christian charity.

Lord Mackay
of Clashfern

James M. Campbell

Introduction

❊❊❊

Fifty years ago Blythswood Care's Founder the late Jackie Ross was confronted with a question, *'It's all very well for you to be preaching every weekend, but what are you doing for those in need on the streets of Glasgow?'*

That question changed his life. Jackie realised the importance of meeting people at their point of need. Touching lives with simple acts of kindness helps everyone to understand the love of Jesus. What better example is there than the Saviour. He reached out to people in so many practical ways: providing food and water, healing and restoration and recognising physical need as well as spiritual need.

I had the privilege of working alongside Jackie for four years before he died. During that time I began to appreciate his compassion for people regardless of colour, creed or religious background. He simply wanted to help.

The experiences we have growing up shape our lives, even if we don't realise it. I was brought up in very privileged circumstances by loving Christian parents. I often arrived home from primary school to find one of the local down-and-out worthies sitting in our porch enjoying a bowl of my mother's home made broth. He would sometimes go away not only well fed, but wearing a pair of my father's favourite shoes or one of his jackets! That simple act of kindness helped me to understand a little of Jackie's vision for helping those in need.

And he was confident that helping was the right thing to do. God's provision for Blythswood's work was 'wonderful' – a description I heard Jackie use time and again. Psalm 139 reflects that sentiment in verse 14: *'Wonderful are your works; my souls knows it very well.'* I remember one day George Dunn, our Finance Controller at the time, informed me that we had received a gift of 30,000 Deutsche Marks – an unusual gift. He did not know what it was for. Two days later, I received a call from Vasile Pop (whose story you can read in chapter five) excitedly announcing he had secured a plot of land in Dej for building his Kindergarten. The only problem was that it would cost 30,000DM. What a wonderful provision!

In this book you will read many other inspiring stories of ordinary people being used in extraordinary ways. Each one wonderfully illustrates how redemption transfigures every day events and how the Holy Spirit inspires practical down-to-earth spirituality. Who you are, what you are doing and even where you are going really matters to the Lord.

Blythswood Care could not have achieved so much if it were not for the wonderful partners with whom God has linked us, not only in Eastern Europe, but in Asia, Africa and at home here in the UK. It is such a privilege to be a small part of a much bigger plan, and truly humbling to meet so many giants of faith.

Samuel Nimubona was one such man. He had a big heart and an extraordinary vision to bring peace and reconciliation to his beloved Burundi. Every time I spoke to Samuel my day lit up. He was such a warm, loving and caring man, who by God's grace helped many to see the love of Jesus changing their lives. Tragically, his life was cut short in September 2002, but Delphine his wife carries on the work of World Outreach Initiatives today. You can read her story in chapter eleven.

It has been such an encouragement to see our Daniel Centre and Talita Kum projects develop over the last fifteen years under the management of our two Romania Directors, Balazs and Adrian. Their stories are also told in this book.

The final chapter describes Finlay Mackenzie's faith journey and how he was persuaded by Jackie to devote his life to support our many projects and partners in Eastern Europe through working as our Project Manager. It is amazing how the Lord uses so many different experiences and life skills in his service. Finlay's love for tractors and snowploughs has now extended to fire engines and ambulances. His passion is not restricted to emergency vehicles, but has extended to sharing the love of Jesus to all he has the opportunity to preach to at home and abroad. That's the most important passion of all!

We are extremely grateful to all our loyal supporters with whose faithful support we are able to touch the lives of so many people in need all around the world, and to see lives transformed through Christian care for body and soul.

It is our prayer that you will not only read this book and enjoy it, but will be richly blessed by it – as we have been, working alongside these ordinary yet special people who trust in a wonderful God.

'*So if there is any encouragement in Christ, any comfort from love, and participation in the Spirit, any affection and sympathy, complete my joy by being of the same mind, having the same love, being in full accord and of one mind. Do nothing out of selfish ambition or conceit, but in humility count others more significant than yourselves. Let each of you look not only to his own interests, but also to the interests of others.*' PHILIPPIANS 2:1-4

JAMES M. CAMPBELL
Chief Executive
Blythswood Care

Vio Jorza

1

Wonderful – the story of Vio Jorza and Children for Christ, Romania

I was brought up in a village near Arad in Romania. We were a poor family living in a poor village. My parents didn't have enough money to let me go to high school in Arad. I would have needed to stay at the school because of the distance and there was no money for that. But I was a very determined person and was totally focussed on going to school and university. I say I was determined, but maybe it was more that I was a fighter, a survivor.

When I was 14 years old I went to the school in Arad and asked to speak to the director. I think she might have been surprised at my visit.

'Here I am,' I said. 'I have come to take the school's entrance exam. But, if I pass the exam, I will need an allowance to keep me while I am here. I am very poor and cannot survive without an allowance.'

'You are very courageous for a 14 year old,' the director replied. 'You take the exam and let's see how you get on.'

I sat the exam and, when the results were known, I had come fifth from the top of the list. Once again I went to see the director.

'This is my result,' I said. 'I have come fifth on the list. Now can I have an allowance to become a boarding pupil at your school?'

She was probably surprised at how well I had done.

'I think so,' she said.

The director argued my case and said that, because I had come in very good time, I should get a full allowance, meaning all my expenses would be paid. That year there was a system of reducing costs for poor pupils, and there were some really poor people in Romania then. It was unusual for a pupil of my age to get a full allowance at that school. I could never have gone there without it.

Home versus school

My father was a Christian who learned to read through reading the Bible. When I was young I didn't realise what hard work that must have been and that, although he was not educated, he must have been very clever. My mother was not educated either.

Dad read Bible stories to me and my brother. I remember him trying to teach me about Daniel and the lions' den. It was an interesting story but I didn't understand that it also had a meaning. I didn't take any message from it although Dad tried to tell it in a way to give me the message. Part of me didn't want to understand. You see, I admired my school teachers because they were educated. I looked up to them. At that time in Romania we were brainwashed at school. We were taught that there was no God. Because my teachers were educated and Dad was not, I thought that they must be right. He said that God existed; my teachers said he did not, therefore I decided there was no god.

For a long time I believed that my teachers held the truth and I wanted to be like them. As a child I was a Pioneer, a member of the communist youth organisation. The leaders certainly knew how to indoctrinate children. We were all given red scarves that made us feel we belonged together and belonged to the Party. Sometimes we were taken to statues of communist heroes and told stories of what they had done. We were so patriotic, swearing allegiance to the Romanian flag and things like that. My teachers were proud and they trained us to be proud to be communists. Dad was so different; he was a humble man.

Dad's story

Dad farmed a small piece of land. He had been a soldier in the Second World War. For a time he was under Russians and for a time under Germans. I remember him telling me how he became a Christian.

'We were in the trenches,' he told me, 'just waiting to be attacked. For the first time in my life I prayed to God. And my prayer was, "If you are God, you will spare my life and let me go back to my children and I will trust you".'

He already had children then although my brother and I had not yet been born.

After that battle Dad had to run for his life; they all had to run for their lives. Later, when he saw his long coat, there were bullet holes in it. His legs were not hurt although he was shot at as he ran. Dad was alive and he saw God. The bullet holes in the coat were a testimony to God protecting not only his legs, but his life. When he saw God, Dad said, 'You must be God and you spared my life.' I can't explain what happened to Dad. I'm just telling what he told me.

Soon after Dad was back in our village an itinerant missionary came and, when he and Dad talked, my father embraced the Christian faith. That day he told the missionary, 'I want to have more children and to give them to the Lord.'

Rebellious

It must have been hard for Dad because my brother and I were prayed for since before we were born and when we grew older we did not believe in God. In fact, I was very rebellious. One memory especially fills me with shame. I remember asking my father, 'How are we blessed? I don't see any blessing here. We are the poorest in the village and you came back from the war with so many wounds.' One of Dad's lungs had been damaged and he used to cough up blood. It was such a difficult time for our family. Mum used to tell us to be good, to be quiet and not to annoy Dad because he might die. 'Tell me one blessing,' I demanded. Dad said, 'My children, you are my blessings and you are very smart.'

Even now that memory of Dad's humility moves my heart. He called us blessings and we were against God. He called us smart and we didn't believe. Dad saw the blessings I could not see; he saw them by faith.

My mother was Orthodox and she didn't allow herself to be challenged by the Christian faith. There was a reason for that. My father and another man in the village were the first Christians there and people looked down on them and despised them. I think that hurt and frightened my mother.

Searching or believing

Mum saw and heard Dad trying to teach us. But my father didn't know how to teach. He used to tell us that we just had to believe rather than search, that 'searching' was what we were taught to do in school. Our teachers instructed us to search ideas, not just believe what we were told. But the truth is that they were indoctrinating us, forcing us to accept their thinking and making it sound silly to believe what our parents said. They were lying to us. The real truth was the opposite of what they said. The Bible tells us to search everything and to take what is good. Even now the memory of my father is so vivid. When people say 'the God of Abraham, Isaac and Jacob,' I say, 'the God of my father.'

I had a friend at high school who was a Christian. At the beginning of every year the teacher used to ask the class who was going to church and who was a 'repenter'. That was the name used for evangelicals. My friend had to stand up and say, 'I am.' I admired her. She took me to her church and

I was overwhelmed because there were so many people there. Although I was a very curious girl I didn't go back.

Working through university

People said I was smart and I was often first in the class. What they didn't know was that I was determined to learn and become rich, to get away from our grinding poverty. But when I left school I hit the same old problem again, there was no money for me to go to university. Mum had died and I stayed with my sister in Arad. There was a children's home across the road and I went there to speak to the director. After I told her about my life, and that I loved children and needed to work to get through university, she said she'd take me on trial for a few days. I worked hard and she employed me. Starting at the lowest level, I cared for children and went to university at the same time. Later I became a teacher and after that a speech therapist in the same institution. I was there for many years.

The missing piece

Having thought that university would fulfil my life, it was so empty. Something was missing. Then I met a young man who played in the philharmonic orchestra in Arad. We were married and I thought this would fill my life. But after a year, when I was in my third year at university, I discovered he was homosexual. In Romania that was a criminal offence and he could have been put in prison. I did not want that. I was crushed in all areas of my life when we split up and then divorced.

On Christmas Day 1986 I was a very sad person. Looking out the window of my sister's home I saw a cross on Speranța Church and watched as many people went in. They all looked so happy and I wondered why. In desperation I decided to go to church but the building was so full I couldn't find a seat. As people knew I was a stranger they made a place for me at the front. I felt so ashamed and couldn't even raise my eyes when the sermon started. It was about Jesus, how he came into the world. I felt so guilty that I'd wasted my life by not believing Dad. Crying tears of shame and joy at the same time, I discovered that there is a God, that there was a way out of my misery and desperation. From that time I went to church, turned to God and started reading the Bible. It was such a joy to discover the truth of it.

Make something beautiful

As I had never read the Bible before it was a new world opening to me. Such joy filled my heart and it was the beginning of my new life. I remember praying, 'Lord, you are God. You have power. You see my life is broken. (I pictured a broken vase.) You can take it. You can make something for your glory. I promise I will obey you even when I don't understand.' I challenged God to make something beautiful from my life, promising I would obey him.

Before long I wanted to be baptised but the orphanage was near the church and that was a problem for me. I prayed, 'Oh Lord, all my colleagues will see me here when I get baptised and they will laugh and look down on me.' A day or two before my baptism the orphanage was closed because of an epidemic. It was closed to disinfect the building and nobody was there. That day 85 people were baptised as there was revival in Romania then.

Underground ministry

After I gave my testimony in front of the church a lady working in the Sunday school came straight up to me. She said, 'I feel you should work in Sunday school. We need people there and you are the right person.' Because God gave me a love for boys and girls I knew from the beginning that the call of my life was to work with children. We had regular checks from the government because it was against the law to teach children about Christianity. They said we could sing with them but not teach the Bible. We were doing an underground ministry and, when they came to check, we just stopped what we were teaching and started singing.

I remember one Easter day we had a lesson about Jesus on the cross with flannel boards. A lady came rushing in and said, 'Gather everything. The checking is here.' We had to take everything down and start singing! I also began to organise camps for children away from the town, in secret, in hiding. The other lady teacher lost her job because she gave someone Christian literature. I didn't lose my job because nobody wanted to work in the orphanage. It was a humble job.

A tragic place

Working in the orphanage was very difficult. We had four dorms with twenty children in each. As it was usually one nurse and one carer for twenty children we hardly managed to change their nappies, feed them and then start again. There was no time to cuddle the children, no time to work with them. As we didn't have carpets to put them on, they couldn't walk, they couldn't move anywhere. They were in beds with no toys, with no stimulation.

Years later, when I was a speech therapist, there was a doctor who was a Christian. The pair of us prayed that the Lord would change life for the children in the orphanage. We believed that communism would stay for ever; we couldn't imagine it collapsing. But we prayed that the Lord would change things and give us the opportunity to do something for these children, to really help them. When the revolution came, that building was taken over by an English believer and it became a Christian home for a time.

Revolution!

In December 1989 I heard that something was happening in Arad and went with others to see what it was. I saw with my own eyes tanks and soldiers and massive crowds of people coming from factories. And I cried when youngsters going from factories walked hand in hand toward the tanks, thinking they would all die. I prayed that the Lord would turn things when the mass of people arrived at the tanks. One of the youngsters had flowers and climbed on a tank and gave the flowers to the soldiers. Perhaps he said that we were all Romanians and wanted peace. Nothing happened. No cruelty. No fires.

Somebody came and called for the people's attention and then asked us to pray the Our Father prayer. Everything stopped and everyone knelt down in front of the town council to pray. Pastors climbed on to a platform made especially for them, made spontaneously, and they preached that God exists. It was overwhelming. To say God exists while Ceausescu was still living! That could have cost lives. God's hand was over us because nobody died that day. That was the first day of the revolution in Arad.

What now?

After the revolution a new world opened and I felt I had to do ministry but didn't know what I should do. For a time I was director of a Christian orphanage but soon felt that God was calling me into evangelising children. That's when I met Wilma and Harry Somerville in the orphanage. They came with a team from Aberdeen in Scotland to change the kitchen. According to Wilma, it was like the Black Hole of Calcutta. She brought some materials for Sunday school and asked who was interested. Of course the people said, 'Vio is.' I was just back from a visit to the Republic of Moldova. We went there to teach children but ended up teaching Sunday school teachers. They had no resources at all.

It was very difficult to see the lack of materials and the indoctrination which was even stronger in the Republic of Moldova than in Romania. Of course, we understood that perfectly and they begged us to go back. I prayed, saying, 'Lord if you want us to go back, give us something in our hands to give them. We cannot go there with empty hands.' Then, on my return, I met Wilma and Harry. When we met in the kitchen Harry, who was a plumber, was under a sink. As I began to tell him about the Republic of Moldova, and how things were there, Harry started to cry. He was dirty and the tears made a mark on his face. I'll never forget that. 'We have to help,' he told Wilma. It felt as though a connection had been made that came from heaven.

The first lorry

The next day Wilma came with me to a Bible club we had in a small village near Arad. Even though we had just met we felt like family and prayed together. Within three weeks of leaving Romania Wilma came back with a lorry full of Sunday school materials transported by Blythswood. That was the first lorry coming with materials including 150 flannel boards. We organised some training in Romania and after that we went to the Republic of Moldova. That was years and years ago and from that beginning came the ministry Children for Christ.

A new ministry

Children for Christ started in 1993 in Romania. Before that we took girls and boys away in secret to camps and taught them about the Lord Jesus Christ. Many of them became Christians. We used to dream about having a place of our own for a campsite and after the revolution we prayed that God would give us such a place, and he did – a piece of land in the foothills of Romanian West Carpathians. At the same time a church from Portlethen in Scotland gave us a portable hall which they had used for their Sunday school. As we didn't have money to transport it to Romania, Harry spoke on the radio about this need. A lady, who was widowed, offered to give us the necessary money. Her act of generosity was in memory of her husband. We met this lady fifteen years later at a deputation meeting in Scotland. What a joy! The camp has been running all these years bringing many children to Christ.

I was an unlikely person for God to use to arrange camps because I have had problems with my hip from childhood. That was one reason I wanted to be educated as I knew I could not do physical work, yet here I was organising camps for children and young people. Over the years hundreds of children, perhaps thousands, have been to Christian camps and hundreds have trusted in the Lord. We hear how they are getting on from all over the world, even from America. Not long ago we heard of someone being baptised who came to the Lord for the first time at camp. That's beautiful!

My brother

I rejoice when a child believes in Jesus but my father didn't live to see his child become a Christian as I came to the Lord the year after he died. My brother, who was given to the Lord when he was born, was an alcoholic. He was quite bad, ready to divorce his wife and lose his family. I used to say that there should be a camp for alcoholics. Finally Blythswood found a place for him in a Hungarian camp. My brother is Romanian but his wife is Hungarian and they went to the camp together. It could not have been better as she translated for him.

God is very good and my brother was converted and is now a changed man. It's such a joy to meet him and to know him. He loves the Lord and works with other alcoholics. As well as that he's very, very busy in the church, especially in counselling people. The Lord was following him from his birth. We were both given to God by our father and we belong to him with all our hearts.

Boxes of blessings

I would like to tell you about the Blythswood shoeboxes that come to Romania and to show how much they mean to those who get them. Shoeboxes don't need to be stuffed full to have everything in them. This is what I mean. They all contain some things for the daily routine to remind us that other people care. Each has a calendar for every day. All of them have a book, Christian literature for children or for adults. Many people have never had a gift in their lives. Those who receive them know that a lot of effort has gone into filling the boxes. God works many miracles through small things. Sometimes we don't realise that. We think we have to do big things, but smaller things like shoeboxes are really great and touch so many lives.

A lady told me that her shoebox was the only gift she received for Christmas and she was glad that we didn't forget her. That lady died, but before that I had an opportunity to share the gospel with her through the gift of a shoebox. And the joy they bring to children is great. They are always delighted to get them. One year the children's shoebox book was about Paul's life. Much care went into it and it was very easy to understand.

Many poor families live near our church whose children struggle to have their daily food. Sometimes it's hard for them because they don't have everything they need to go to school. I remember four or five years ago people from Blythswood came to give shoeboxes. We took them to a school in a very poor neighbourhood. As soon as the children received them they took their shoeboxes to the corner of the street and sat down to open them. You can't imagine the joy that was on their faces.

It is the same with the supplies Blythswood gives us for our camps, things like soup. One year we had enough that we were able to give another charity some soup in exchange for something else. Because everything can be turned into a blessing we are grateful for all that is sent out to us. I would like the people who give to Blythswood to know that.

A wonderful God!

How can I sum up my story? I think God answered my father's prayers. He put all the pieces of my life together and it's great to be able to serve such a wonderful God. He fills my life, and not only mine, for he also allows me to share the good news that Jesus is the only Saviour with so many children and with our army of camp leaders. It's wonderful. He is wonderful!

2

Building the future – the story of Charles Ficsor and the Good News Foundation, Hungary

I always believed in God and in his son Jesus Christ even when I was young and at home living with my parents on the farm. I never questioned the existence of Jesus Christ. I always knew for sure that he exists, that he is alive. I can't tell you how and when I became a Christian and I think it was like this because of what I heard from my parents and what I experienced from them. My parents were very special. I was a boy just at the end of the Second World War and I noticed that they never complained about the Russians even when other people did and even when they were treated very badly.

In those days, if someone had grown a crop, the leaders wanted it. They didn't buy it; they just took it. We were told that it belonged to the Soviet Union and the Soviets took our crops because they were helping us. One year, after we cut the corn and took in the harvest, we had a pile left out in the field that we covered up. Somebody's pigs broke loose and they found our corn and began to eat it. The owner of the pigs went to the local government official saying that we were hiding our corn. Immediately the police came and took it away. My father too was taken and was put in prison. That was in 1952 when I was twelve.

Prison

Our mother didn't know what was happening to Dad. She tried to get information but nobody answered. We learned that he was in Orgovány, about five kilometres from our farm. He was beaten up there. Dad had to stand by the wall and a man kicked him in his belly with his boots on. That caused such big problems for his stomach that he had to be operated on and he had stomach trouble even when he died at an elderly age. For Dad's final hearing in front of a judge, my mother was allowed to go and be there. For some reason, I still don't know why, Mum took me with her. We had to go to a nearby village, about eight kilometres away from here. We went by horse cart and left the horses with someone we knew. I remember it very well. We saw Dad. He was standing in the front and, as he wasn't even allowed to turn around, he never saw us.

When the judge asked Dad why he hid the corn, he said, 'We didn't mean to hide it. Our custom is to cover corn after the harvest so that it will dry.' The judge asked for the opinion of people there who were good at agriculture, asking whether it is a good method to dry corn this way. When he asked that question the judge was told that, yes, this is the way to do it. Maybe that was why he wasn't punished even more. We prayed for my dad and God answered us. It was a very big miracle that he was freed because we were considering that he might get hanged or killed. In those times, if the leadership didn't like someone, that could happen.

Fine examples

My father never said a word against his enemies or against God, even when he came home from the prison. I'm very sad that before he died I didn't ask him about his months in prison. We knew he couldn't speak about it at the time, but perhaps he could have told me later on. There was freedom to talk by the time my dad was old, but by then we were used to not asking things.

If there was trouble or problems on the farm, my parents didn't make a big deal of it. I can remember that one year our grape harvest was so poor that we managed to make 100 litres of wine altogether when it would have been natural to make 100 hectolitres. Our vineyard was about three or four kilometres away from the farm and, when an ice storm came in 1954, I remember my father saying, 'Let's go and see.' We saw all the damage that the hail had done and still my father didn't complain. He considered the situation for a little while and then said, 'Tomorrow we will go again and we will sprinkle the vineyard with fertiliser.' I said, 'What's the point? Everything is ruined.' He said,

'Son, we are building the future.' I learned a lot from my father that day.

Teenage years

I was 14 years old at the time and by then I had memorised a great many verses of scripture. There was not one verse that was very special to me; all of the Bible was special. The verses I memorised all those years ago are still in my memory today. The following year I was baptised. I wanted everyone to know I was a Christian.

At the age of fourteen I finished primary school. In those times if you had lands to work, you were considered a class alien and thus your children were not accepted to attend secondary school. In 1956 things started to change and we realised that even I would be allowed to go and study. When I was nineteen-years-old my father went to the authorities and asked if I could go and learn to work with steel. That happened to be market day. When he came home Dad said to me, 'In two days' time, on Saturday, you will go and work for this man.' I said, 'Yes, if my father says so, I will go.' So I went to a vocational school to learn from that man's workmanship.

Young soldier

When I was still in the first year of vocational school a teacher asked me why I didn't go to high school. I explained that I couldn't because my father was a peasant farmer with fields. A few weeks later he came back to me and said, 'Son, you have to go and study in a high school.' So while I did my second year at vocational school, I also did the first year of high school. I went to both schools at the same time. Just before I finished that year I was enrolled to go for my compulsory soldier years.

After a time I was given permission to leave the base every Monday evening because I was still studying at high school. I knew it wasn't my commander who let me go to school but it was a gift from God so I could finish my high school education. When I came out the army after twenty-six months I asked for a document proving that I had been mending planes for that time. I thought the documentation might come in useful one day. Then I went back to high school to sit my third and fourth year exams and also took my final exams for the vocational school. After another four years I graduated from college as a mechanical engineer.

I think people knew at school, the army and in college that I was a Christian but I didn't talk much about it. Many times my peers noticed that I wasn't cursing or joining them in saying bad things. We had lessons on atheism but the teachers didn't blame me for my Christianity and the lessons never made me question my faith. When I went home the village Communist Party secretary was very much against me. That was interesting because the Party leader in my college was the teacher I was closest to and he never questioned me in an unpleasant way.

Marriage

In the mid 1960s I had this desire in my heart that I needed a wife and prayed about it every day. In the spring of 1967 the pastor in my church sometimes asked me to give him a lift because I had a car. One day as we drove he asked if I wanted to get married soon. I told him I wasn't sure. During that summer I started thinking about his daughter Agnes. She was sixteen then and I was twenty-six. That autumn, without discussing it with Agnes, I explained to my pastor that I'd like him to ask his daughter if she would marry me. Agnes told me later that, after her father spoke to her, she decided she wouldn't go to sleep until she got an answer from God about the question.

When everybody went to bed, Agnes asked God to give her a verse. A verse was given to her that said that something good will come with this so trust in him in this question. Agnes prayed again and said, 'It's quite an encouraging verse but, Lord, please give me another verse too.' The meaning of the next one that God brought to her mind was very similar. I went to see Agnes on the following Saturday and she said, 'Yes.' We were engaged in October and then married the next year. I'm still as sure as I was then that she is a gift from God to me and she too knows that this marriage is from the Lord. We get on very well and we love each other very much. I told her about two years ago that I love her even more since I was ill (I had strokes in 2013) but she said that I always loved her.

Discerning God's will

Soon after we were married we decided that we would be happy to go and work in a Baptist old people's home in another town. There wasn't a leader there at that time.

Another couple also applied. We were told that, because we were very young and didn't have any children, it was too early for us to work there. The other couple got the job and stayed for fifteen years.

At the beginning of the 1960s I wanted to go to Africa and do some ministry there. When I married Agnes we understood from each other that we both wanted to go to Africa. Because we were in Hungary that just didn't work. Although we weren't allowed to go to other countries, we didn't give up the idea for a long time. In 1973, I went to the United States hoping that I would get into contact with some people who would be able to organise a mission trip to Africa for us. It never happened; I was too old by then. God wanted us at home instead.

For two or three years after we were married I worked on the land. Then I began an engineering job where my boss was the local Party leader. I remember telling him that I didn't go to church because I had to, or because my wife's father was the pastor, I went because I wanted to go. He didn't like me and eventually promoted a newly qualified engineer over me. Months later I saw an advertisement for someone to work at the college where I had studied. I applied and was accepted. It was a well-paid job.

A change of direction

There was a man in charge of the whole college and his deputy and then I was third in line of seniority. In my sixth year of working there I received a letter from the Baptist Union in

Budapest, saying that the Church's retirement home needed a director and they would like me to move there and take the job. We didn't know why they wanted an engineer to run their retirement home. I went for a meeting in Budapest to talk about it. We agreed that this change could happen within a year, not immediately. Then the time came when I had to decide for sure whether or not to go. I had a very good job and was wondering if it was the right thing to leave my high salary and my college job to work in the retirement home. After talking about it with Agnes we agreed to go. The salary in my new job was very low and I didn't ask for it to be raised. We were just happy with whatever they gave us and we were there for nine years.

Three years before we left the retirement home, God showed me that the work we'd been doing there had been well done but that he wanted more from me. He wanted me to work, not only with elderly people, but with all generations. I started sharing my thoughts with those in the retirement home and also in our church. Nobody took me seriously but it was very serious for Agnes and for me. Although my job was not well paid I understood that, if I started the new ministry that was on my mind and in my heart, I wouldn't have a salary at all. Both Agnes and I knew from God that we had to trust him for everything, that we were not to ask people for money. Another two years passed before we were sure that it was the right time to move and start the ministry that God had shown me. That was why I went with my wife and children, Renáta (21), Hella (19), Pálma (18), Lilla (14) and Donát (11) back to Orgovány in the summer of 1991.

Trusting God for everything

Two years after we started trusting in the Lord to provide for all our needs one of my shoes developed a 10 cm long split on the front. That made me wonder if I might have to give up my service and find a paid job. The director of my previous workplace called me and offered a manager's position. I did not say yes, rather I waited because I had asked my Lord for shoes. He really tried me and then sent my brother-in-law who offered me a pair of shoes! During our service we learned how to live in need and in abundance. Since then, I can say with gratefulness to God that I have always had shoes. In the past fifteen years God has used Blythswood Care to supply shoes, clothes, food etc. so our life became carefree.

We all had jobs to do in the church. My eldest was the youth worker and we were all happy to take part in the congregation's life. Nobody asked what we lived on. God led us to start working for the whole country, the whole Hungarian-speaking country, beyond the borders. Then in 1995 we realised that we had to put more energy into the local ministry. It happened like this.

Our daughters and some other young people went to a youth conference and they came home on a Sunday afternoon. We had an evening meeting in the church and our daughter went to see the pastor when the meeting was over. She told him that they had been to a youth conference and were challenged and had responded to the challenge, saying that within a year they would each lead one person to Christ. The pastor said, 'Oh, you should have done this before. It's not a new thing.' So these young people came to see Agnes and me and shared what the pastor had said. I thought he was right but I didn't tell the youngsters. Instead I told them I thought they had to do something and suggested making use of Sunday lunchtimes.

First person saved

We had a meeting at church on Sunday mornings and a meeting in the afternoons but a break at lunch time when we could meet together and pray with them. We agreed to do that and they started coming in the lunch hour. After a few Sundays I said they should consider finding one person each that they wanted to invite to come to Jesus. When a girl said there was someone she knew who was ready to come and see Christian people, we agreed that she would start praying for that very person and the other youngsters would each start praying for someone they knew to become interested. The following Sunday this girl said that her friend had been saved by God. We were very happy. It was a good start. We warned them that maybe this wouldn't happen every week and not to be discouraged if it didn't.

The prayer meetings continued after that. At the end of the summer my wife decided that we should make it possible for those people who were interested in learning about God and the Bible to do that. I started inviting people we had already supported through the Good News Foundation. Most of them were poor and would have had shoes or clothes from us. We advertised locally just by word of mouth, not in a paper, that for six Sunday afternoons we would have a study group where people could come to find out more. The

Good News Foundation is a civil Christian organization that engages in missionary service. Among its important aims are passing on the love of God, reaching down to people in need, refreshing the tired ones, showing the way to those who are lost and giving bright light in the darkness.

Agnes took the leadership at these meetings and, when the fifth Sunday came, I told the people we'd have another meeting the next Sunday and then we'd finish because the six weeks would be gone. One of those who came said, 'Can we continue, please?' I said, 'Oh, yes we can.' That was what we wished. That's how The Good News Club started. The aim of the meeting was to identify people God led us to and then to pray for them to be saved.

Conversions

At first we planned that we would make a list of all the people who were saved but we soon realised that we couldn't do that because people came and went, even from as far away as Transylvania. They would come for a meeting or two and be touched by God and become Christians but we never heard about them after that. Just recently I learned of a man who made a commitment at the meeting whose family come here often. He has now been a Christian for a long time but we only heard about it after twenty years.

We also know about some young people who were saved here. One of them moved to Budapest and another moved somewhere else and they are both active in churches where they are. Recently I received an email from a lady who now lives in Budapest. Her daughter lives in England. They became Christians here and are both going on with the Lord. She mentioned our jubilee meeting that she attended and said that I had the very same smile I had twenty years ago when they started coming to our church!

Local people gave us clothes and shoes to distribute to those in need, but they were always very well worn. Once Raymond Arnold came with SGA; he used to work with Blythswood. 'Do you need any food or clothes or anything? Do you have any needs?' he asked us. I explained that, if something was offered to us, we could accept but that we wouldn't ask. Raymond went from us to Transylvania and then he flew back to Britain. I thought we would never hear from him again, but we did. In June the following year a lorry arrived from Blythswood full of clothes and shoes. For the next two or three years a lorry came in every year. It was a lot of work for us to unload it and there was a problem finding somewhere to store things until we could distribute them. We did find a place and everything that was received was given to someone in need.

So much aid

As well as clothes and shoes Blythswood also sent furniture. Food was delivered too and that was very valuable. One year, three pallets of baby food came along with other kinds of food. It was so much appreciated that people spoke about it for a long time, about how much they loved the baby food and what a great help it was. There were all sorts of different things. We had no idea how Blythswood managed to collect so much aid. There is still great need all around Hungary. We don't only work in this area, or within a twenty or thirty kilometre radius, but we take aid to the north, to the west, to the east and to the south. We have some in the store just now and a reformed pastor is going to collect it for distribution in his area.

I am old now. God is still my shepherd and I don't lack anything. Age brings many problems but I am very happy with it. I'm also happy because I know that my children do a very good job in the ministry. Donat is with the Good News Foundation that I worked with for twenty-five years. That is comforting to me. God is my comfort.

Dragisa Armus

3

I am Mr Dragisa – the story of Dragisa Armus and Blythswood Serbia

I was brought up as one of three children in my family. My sister is much older than me, about twenty years older, and my earliest memory is of her wedding when I was about five years old. She was living in a nearby village and her husband came from another village about seven kilometres away. The Serbian tradition was that she had to go to her marriage on a horse with her friends helping her. That scene has stayed in my mind. That was about 200 kilometres from where I live how. It is in Kosovo; I was brought up in Kosovo. I now live in Vrnjacka Banja.

My background is Orthodox. I don't remember my mother ever visiting a church but my father, who was a road-man, went about once a year. But as far as I know he never entered the church. There was an event there at Christmas or Easter time and he stood outside the celebration along with

all the others who did not go inside. He was not very interested in the ceremony, just in being nearby.

Not even one

In 1956, when I was seven years old, I went to school. I liked
school even when we had to travel to get there in deep snow in
the winter. Very often I didn't have good shoes but I enjoyed
school anyway, even with cold wet feet. When I was a child,
religion was something that was for the past and there was a
totally materialistic view of the world. The slogan we learned
was '*There is no God.*' I grew up knowing no Bible stories at
all, not even one. Maybe I had seen crucifixes on some historic
monasteries but they meant nothing to me, they were just to
do with old and pointless traditions.

Once a year we had a holiday on a saint's day and we
had to take special bread called Slava cake to the priest to
be placed in my home village of Ljevosa. The saint was St
John, Slava, and his day was 20th January. I was given a little
money to take for the priest's dedication of Slava cake. That
was my job. As a child we celebrated Christmas but only with
special food. It was not a religious celebration, nothing to do
with the birth of Christ. It was the same at Easter. We had
painted eggs but didn't know they had anything to do with
Jesus rising from the dead.

Deep thoughts

Although we were told nothing about Jesus, in my mind I was
thinking about things. It was in the elementary school, before

middle school, I started thinking that there must be something eternal. I thought a lot about eternity at that time. In my mind, without anybody to tell me, and with no Bible in my hand, I imagined that there must be eternity and also that there is life that is the opposite of eternity. I saw people were dying and my question all the time was: we are here for a time and then is the end, so what about eternity? I seemed to know that eternity is time without end. That was a burden to me because I didn't know how to find an answer.

I heard from my mother that I had six brothers and sisters whom I never saw. They died because there was at that time all kind of diseases that children caught. They lived one year or two years, and all before I was born. That was why I was such a small child at the time of my sister's marriage. Perhaps it was knowing about my dead brothers and sisters that put thoughts of eternity in my mind when I was too young to really think about these things.

School was solid; it was strict. The teacher disciplined us by hitting us with a special stick. You had to stretch your hands out and the teacher would strike. It was normal; it was not good. I was from a village and the teacher knew my mother. She ordered her wooden stick from my mother and I was obliged to take it to the classroom. With that stick I was often struck and I didn't like it. That was normal and accepted then. It does not happen now.

My middle school was the school of economics. I liked typography – machine typing without looking. I was good at that work. We also studied economy but that was not special. Our eight years of elementary school was followed by middle school for four years. After that came the time to make big decisions about life.

Searching for truth

I was still troubled about eternity and started drinking and listening to loud music. Maybe I was trying to suppress the voice from inside which gave me questions but no answers. It was in 1966 when, with my friends and relatives, I went on a visit home to Ljevosa. There I met my cousin Simo Ralevic who was a fairly newly converted man. I think he might have been in theological school by then. He was nine years older than me.

We started a Bible study and that was when I first saw a New Testament. For two years I went to the Bible study from time to time, not often. Although I was still not a Christian I would argue against those who opposed Christianity. At one Bible study the subject was time, eternity and the end of time. It was so graphic that it hit my stony heart and mind hard enough for them to open and for me to understand. I saw eternity and Jesus in the centre of that eternity. Then the Holy Spirit brought my conversion which I simply experienced as a moving from above. All that combined to help me to understand about eternity and about Jesus Christ and the reason for his birth, death and resurrection.

After that I could say with inspiration and joy to my friend Cedo, 'From now I am a Christian.' And I remember the words he said. 'You know Dragisa, now the angels in heaven are rejoicing.' For me, a nineteen-year-old, there was great joy to know that the angels were rejoicing.

When I told my parents that I had become a Christian my father was just silent. I think he was converted because he was never opposed to it and he read the Bible. My mother in the beginning liked what happened in my life and was not against it. She prepared food when Simo came to celebrate my conversion. Later she opposed my baptism and so on, but she changed somehow after that. Then I could witness to her. Before she died, when she was ninety-three, I often asked her about her faith and, when I explained the way of salvation, she said that she believed.

A difficult time

I started my eighteen months army service the same month I was converted. Illegally I had a small New Testament that I put in my drawer every evening, and every morning I put it in my pocket. After eighteen months it had left a stamp on the lining of my pocket but it was never found. The punishment would have been harsh if it had been. I could, from time to time, not often, read some verses. 'I am the way, the truth and the life' (John 14:6) was one of my favourite verses at the very beginning because I had found the truth. I remember that very clearly.

As I was a very young believer it was hard to be without church and without Christian fellowship. I shared my faith with my friends in the army when possible. Although I liked to share, it was not easy as I had no older Christians to help me grow. In 1970 I left the army and then faced the choice about what to do with my life. One possibility was to go and work in Germany. West Germany was asking for workers and I prepared all the papers to go. But very firm in my mind at the time was the call, because I felt it very strongly, to consecrate myself to something that had value for eternity. That's why I decided to go to mission school, Bible school. There was a Bible school in Novisad.

Future plans

My parents disliked this idea and were very opposed to it. They wanted me to go to Germany where a job was waiting, where there would be money. The struggle inside was very strong. Eventually I tore up my papers for Germany and made the decision to start Bible school. The next years were full of study. After four years in Bible school I decided to study some more because I was single and free. So I went for another four years to the philology faculty of Skopje University. While I was studying there I attended a church about 150 kilometres away every weekend for the whole weekend of meetings. Even when I was studying in Skopje I was always involved in mission work.

I studied language and literature, English and American literature, morphology and many other subjects. All students were obliged to read part of the New Testament because they couldn't study Milton, Shakespeare or Bunyan's Pilgrim's Progress without knowledge of the Bible. When I once offered New Testaments as gifts to everybody, thinking they might take them to study their university subjects, the professor said they didn't like such propaganda.

After graduating from Skopje in 1978 I went back to Pec. I was not involved in any specific missionary organisation; I just worked and witnessed to spread the gospel. Much of the time that was done by visiting people. If someone called from Croatia or Bosnia or Montenegro, I went there together with some brothers. Brother Simo was often with me. The people we visited contacted us through our literature and knew our church address from that. If they got in touch with us, we were happy to travel long distances to visit them.

The gospel in print

At that time we printed some tracts with a simple gospel message. Simo was busy in Pec printing many different booklets and sending them to people by post. We also went out in the streets and distributed literature, for example, in Montenegro. Montenegro was especially atheistic. We took our rucksacks packed with Christian materials and travelled by bus to different places. When we arrived we stepped out in towns or villages and shared New Testaments and booklets. There were three of us in the team then, Simo, Cedo and me. After two years doing that I moved to Banja.

Banja was a potential new mission field because it was a tourist place and there was no church. I spent 20 per cent of the time there and 80 per cent of the time travelling all around Yugoslavia, not Slovenia. My focus was Montenegro and the Dalmatian coast. Some people joke with me about that because Nada, who became my wife, was there. I met Nada on the mission field. She was a Christian from a Catholic background and somehow I came in contact with her. Nada and one brother especially used to come to our Bible studies. We did not work for money. Our support came from many different places: individuals, missions, churches and from different countries too. God took care of all that.

We were heavily involved in the crisis after the war in 1991. I'll never forget preaching the Word and doing humanitarian work in Central and South Serbia, Kosovo and Bosnia. Among the places we worked were Vrnjacka Banja, Kraljevo, Trstenik, Krusevac, Krgujevac, Pec, Sarajevo and Sokolac. Millions of pieces of literature were distributed.

In 1999 my mother and other family members had to leave their homes in Ljevosa, three kilometres from Pec. One morning they saw that there was nobody left in the village. They started to go and somehow I knew about the situation. Everybody was leaving at five in the morning and I went into the room about that time and told my wife I was going to Kosovo. Within fifteen minutes I was in the car. I found them in their village. My mother had her belongings in a wheelbarrow. She had refused to leave until then because she had lived there for ninety years. When I found my family beside the road I put them in the car and brought them to my home in Banja.

Ethnic issues

My own family covered both sides of the conflict. I am a Serb from Kosovo and my wife Nada is Croatian. During all the troubles we had to act as Christians and not show any bitterness towards people from other ethnic groups. Even today I call all Christian people, whatever their background, to show the unity we all have in Christ. A few months ago I invited Brother Essat, who is from Albania, to come and preach in my church in Albanian.

The town of Pec is on top of a hill. You can see it very clearly. There is a church there. The people there told me, 'You know the church comes to this spot every week and we pray under the statement that "God loves Pec".' So there is a regular church there and the worshippers are Albanian brothers and sister, new believers. God's Word is not preached in vain. For example, I knew Montenegro when it was almost totally atheistic. Now there are believers here and there and people are gathering in groups; churches are being opened. The number of Christians in Croatia and Serbia is growing too.

My heart's desire

Since 1991 we have gone to Serbia, Bosnia and Montenegro to do humanitarian work. For the last seventeen years we've done a great deal there with Blythswood Care. I would like to visit the people more, to be involved in the work of church planting. My heart's desire is to evangelise, to fill many towns with the gospel, to open churches that will bear testimony to people in towns, villages and the countryside.

Sometimes, even when we were doing humanitarian work, life was very dangerous. I will tell you one story of what happened in Bosnia. I was arrested and held for eight hours. For the first six hours I thought it was just a routine check. Then they took my personal Bible and looked at it for half an hour, especially at the notes I had written in it in tiny writing. They were looking for a secret code! In their eyes I was an American spy. Then, during the last two hours, I felt something different that I can't explain. I had left my wife and four small children at home and was there on my own. The man who was guarding me told me not to move. Their idea was to kill me. One bullet, finito. The General was informed and he came to see the spy before they killed me.

The General came. Somebody welcomed him and said his name, 'Mr C', and I remembered it was the man I had received many thank-you letters from! I had letters from him in my drawer at home. We had sent humanitarian help for children, for the whole town, including school materials and so on, and I had letters thanking me from this same man! When I heard his name I stood up and said, 'Mr C, I am Mr Dragisa. I have your thank-you letters.' Before I said that he was cursing. After I told him who I was, he stopped. His first question was, 'Can I have a Bible?' I had a package of twenty-four Bibles and I stooped down to get one. Can you imagine? That was the happiest thing, handing him a Bible. It was one of the happiest times of handing over a Bible in my life.

After that I was asked many questions about permissions, about saints, about Christmas, Easter and Ascension holidays. The end of the story is that I persuaded them it was a big rumour that I was a spy, a false rumour just to kill me and be free of me. The General could see that it was not true. Ten days later they invited me to a big celebration, a banquet with a large number of people at it. After that we continued to go there and do missionary work. Being put in prison didn't stop us. In fact, it helped us to continue to go to Bosnia.

A sound investment

Serbia is a country that needs to hear the gospel. People do not know who Jesus is. I think it's time for Serbia to be evangelised more and more. We have towns and villages without any gospel and they need more investment. Kragujevac is nearby and in need of investment, spiritual investment, prayer investment. Vranje is a place with 70,000 people without God and without the Bible.

I met one family there. After I shared the gospel, I asked them to hear the Bible as I read it to them. Then the lady said, 'Listen to my husband and what he will tell you.' I wondered what he would say. It turned out that his grandfather was Justin Popovic, the famous and reliable theologian. I met him as a young believer and I have all his books. He was localised by the communists and not free to move around. Justin Popovic had to stay in a monastery because they were afraid of his influence. The communists localised many speakers and writers; they tried to hide them, to silence them. The man who was speaking to me was the grandson of the great Justin Popovic, but he didn't have a Bible. I gave one to him.

There is a special tradition in Orthodox churches. People can become 'friends' or 'godfathers' of a church for a year and many believe that, if they do, God will especially bless them.

People offer bids for the privilege and it goes to the highest bidder. There was a poor woman in Vranje whose child was sick. At the time of bidding she said, 'Please, I have only 400 Euros to give. Please let me be the friend or godfather of this church and God will bless my sick child. Please don't bid against me.' There was a big crowd of people there. One man, who had a special ring, offered 700 Euros. Then someone else offered 1,000 Euros and that person's bid was accepted. He became the friend or godfather of the church. That sad story makes me want to evangelise that poor woman.

This is happening in Serbia today. Today Serbia really, really needs much investment in evangelisation, much investment in prayer. Whenever I get the opportunity I say that to people and I want to say it in this book. Please pray for Serbia.

Besa Shapllo

4

The first Amen – the story of Besa Shapllo and Mission Possible Albania

I was born in Tirana, Albania, but lived in Durres for fifteen years before coming back to Tirana for middle school and university. We were three children: my brother, my sister and I, and we had a happy childhood for our parents were very caring and loving.

In 1968 Albania proclaimed itself atheist and closed down all religious institutions including churches. No one was allowed to even whisper the word 'God'. Sometimes young women who were wearing a necklace with the cross, not necessarily because they were believers, but because they liked the symbol, were stopped by the police and taken to a police station, not imprisoned, just to scare them.

God was not mentioned in school. However I remember a conversation with a classmate when I was about nine years old. She insisted that God existed while I said there was no

God. Then she asked, 'But who makes the figs sweet?' and I had no answer. There was no mention of God in our home. My parents were members of the Communist Party, although by mother's background was Orthodox and my father's Bektashi which is Sunni Muslim, but very liberal.

Later I went to the capital to attend a high school specialising in languages, to study English. I don't remember much that is important and interesting about school, but my diary tells me a strange thing. Although we Albanians didn't believe in God, over and over again in my diary from these years I wrote, 'God help me.' That was written again when I was at university and afterwards. I don't know what my mind was thinking. And I certainly was not happy in 1974 when I wrote, 'World is empty. World and life are nothing. No joy. No gaiety. Only despair. Only boredom, depression, gloom, clouds, emptiness.'

A hidden gun

While I was at school and university I worked as a tour guide in tourist hotels in the summer, speaking to the tourists in English. There was an atheist museum that I took tourists to visit and I saw a Bible there, the first I had ever seen. It was a big Bible and it lay open. The inside was cut out and a gun had been placed in the hollow. The whole exhibition was about trials of Catholic priests. Some of the tourists did not come inside the museum. I always wondered why they refused. Maybe they were Christians. I used to be given important Friends of the Communist Party to take round, Marxist-Leninists from other countries.

My first journey outside Albania was in 1989 when I went to Greece. At that time we weren't allowed to travel abroad as we are free to travel now. Those few who could travel had to complete many forms and answer many questions to see if they would be allowed to leave the country. The first time I was interviewed I told the official that a friend of my mother had invited me. The two women had been together in a concentration camp in the Second World War in Germany. I was not given permission to go at first, but then I was.

Raw potatoes

My mother had been a partisan with a partisan unit in the south east of Albania. The Germans were behind this unit and there was a big ditch between them. As Mum was small like me she could not jump the ditch and she was caught along with seven others. First they took them to Thessalonica in Greece and from there to Germany. After the war ended they were freed but they had no food to eat. There were nine women together and one of them sold a ring for nine potatoes that they ate raw. They were so hungry. My mother was not quite eighteen years old when she came back after more than a year in the concentration camp. That was a terrible experience but it opened my mother's mind through meeting people from other countries.

When I was in my last year at university, my friends and I did our annual compulsory month of military training and teased each other that none of us had a boyfriend. It was during that month that I met Agron, who later became my husband. I think both of us felt that our relationship was something that would go well to the end. I took Agron to meet my parents. That wasn't the custom in Albania at the time as most people had arranged marriages. My parents had a love marriage after they met through the Communist Party. Agron and I were married in 1977. All my family were Party members except myself. My father said he hoped he would see me be a member before he died. Agron became a Party member ten years after we married. A group of specialist engineers from where he worked were going to Italy for six months and, if you were not a party member, you could not go.

Hard times

I taught English in an elementary school for four years and then went to teach in a school that specialised in foreign languages. During the last years of communism life became even worse in Albania – no food, empty, closed shops. Things were happening as they are happening in Europe just now with people escaping from their countries to try to find freedom and safety. So many Albanians were fleeing from their homeland, just grasping ships. There were cases of 10,000 people in one ship, packed together like sardines, and some died before reaching Italian shores. Nearly everybody wanted to leave Albania. There was a freedom that was never given to Albanians and people just wanted to see what was on the other side.

Things began to change in 1991 and Agron and I were able to go to New Zealand. In fact, we left the country just when Albania opened up. That sounds as if we were living in a closed box and that is what it was like. We were invited by friends from New Zealand, who had come several times to our country and were called Friends of the Party, let's say Marxist-Leninists. They even asked whoever was in power in the Foreign Office at the time, if we could have permission to go and they would not allow us. So even though they were Friends of the Party, they did not have enough influence. Then in 1991 they repeated their invitation and we were able to go.

An amazing thing

Agron and I came back in May and I think that was the darkest time of all in Albania, though some things had changed. There was one amazing sight to me. On the wall of the tallest hotel in Albania was written, 'Learn English through the Bible.' I had only seen two Bibles, the one in the museum and one in New Zealand. I don't think our friends were believers but it was the custom that everybody should have a Bible, an English Bible. Through our friends I met a Maori lady and she was the first person to speak to me about Jesus and God. I couldn't understand a thing she said but, when I returned home, the first thing that came in the mail from New Zealand was a letter from this lady with a New Testament. I didn't pay much attention to it back then.

However, I wrote to the address on the wall of the hotel. Even before the answer came I met the former President of Mission Possible. This is how it happened. The start of the school year was delayed and we had a friend from New Zealand staying with us. One day I went to the school to collect my salary. An American couple were visiting the school and their guide / interpreter was a pupil of mine and he introduced us. I joined them to tour the school.

'Why do you work here rather than seeking another position?' the American asked, and then suggested I could work in the American Embassy, which was just across the street. I told him that I loved teaching; I loved what I was doing. He said he'd ask if there was a position at the Embassy. I thought that was very strange. The man was staying at the Tirana Hotel, the one with the advertisement.

An evening or two later, Agron and I took our New Zealand friend to see an opera, which was just a two minute walk from that hotel. We hadn't planned a meeting, but we did meet the American couple. Albanians generally are very friendly and we invited the couple to our home. When they came to visit, he brought a lot of books that didn't make an impression on me. They were New Testaments, maybe Bibles, Christian books that I had no idea about. After that we met several times and talked.

The first amen

One day we were in the lobby of their hotel and he was talking about Jesus and God. He asked if I was ready to become a Christian. I said, 'How?' because I didn't realise how to accept Jesus into your life. He said, 'Give me your hands.' I was excited. 'Let's bow our heads,' he said, and then he prayed for me to accept Jesus into my life. At the end he said, 'Amen.' That was the first amen that I said in my life. From that day everything really changed for my life. We were having dinner one night when our American friend said to me, 'Would you like to work for us?' I didn't know anything about his work!

That is how I came to work for Mission Possible, but it was complicated. First I had to make contact with different ministries: the Ministry of Culture, the Ministry of Education and other authorities like that. Mission Possible brought me a fax machine and a computer to put in my office, which was a corner in our bedroom. The first event I had to arrange was at Christmas 1991. Five Christian professors came from the US and we had the biggest – at that time – conference with all the education leaders from Albania. That was organised through the Ministry of Education. Of course, all the speakers were Christians, but they didn't speak about God to these leaders, but about leadership in education. It was very well reported in the newspapers at the time.

The first missionaries started coming to my homeland about then. I became a member of the first church, the Emmanuel Church, where we had an American pastor who had been in Kosovo and spoke Albanian fluently. He and his family lived very close to us. People didn't have phones then, but I had a phone and the pastor would come and use it. I began to become acquainted with the Bible. Everything started to make sense in my whole being, not only in my mind.

Interesting conversations

I also learned to pray, though really I had been praying in a way for nearly twenty years. In my diaries, right back as far as 1974, I wrote 'God Almighty, help me.' Whenever I was in need I would turn to God with that prayer even though I didn't know he existed. That prayer was not only in my diary, it was in my head and in my heart as well. I can only say that it came from the Holy Spirit. It was a strange thing, but even by denying God the Albanian authorities showed that he was there. For example, Albanian television would not translate the word 'God'. Once, in the 1980s, Agron and I discussed this and decided that perhaps the authorities were so much afraid of God that they didn't even translate the word that spelled his name. We were not Christians, and we didn't know I would become a Christian, but even then that seemed strange to us.

We had another conversation, I think in the late 1980s, about the possibility of Albania opening up and about what we'd like to see happen. Both of us were pro-Christian. Why? We didn't know the Bible; we didn't know anything, but the people that we had met from a Christian background seemed good. We had a high opinion of these people, not because they spoke to us about God (no one could speak about God), but because we felt they were better people, nicer people than the rest. We asked ourselves, 'Who was it that brought civilisation to Europe?' We knew that the answer was Christians and therefore we considered them more advanced than anyone else. But we didn't understand about God.

Reactions

Agron went with me to different churches when Albania opened up, but he has never gone regularly. He agrees with what I am doing, but it is for me to do it, not for him. When we were in the United States for the first time in 1993, the former president of Mission Possible took us both to many churches and many families. I shared a lot with the people there. In Chicago a pastor spent time with Agron. He prayed for my husband and told him that one day he would be a pastor. That day has not come. He is a sweet and helpful man to me.

I don't remember much reaction from my teaching friends when I became a Christian and some of them are still my friends. One came to visit me because her husband, a teacher, is a drunkard, and her son has taken to drugs as well. She was so filled with worry that she came just to talk. We spent a lot of time together and I invited her to pray. I'm sure she talked to me and not to another friend because she knows I'm a Christian. She knew she'd find some support and comfort.

I could not go into my parents' hearts to know what they thought of me being converted, but they never said a word. Once, when a missionary and another friend visited our home and prayed for my family, I could see my mother's tears. I think it was hard for that generation to open their mouths to thank God, or even to speak about God, because of what they had grown used to, what they were taught all their lives. In their hearts I have no doubt that they believed in God. How do I know this? It's because I got permission from my father to ask the missionaries to visit; I didn't just invite them myself. My parents made them most welcome in their home. They were proud of me. If they had been against the Lord, they would not have been proud, they would have been ashamed.

Mission Possible

My work with Mission Possible was very varied. In 1992 we started receiving aid from Mission East in Denmark and since 1999 a lot has come from Blythswood in Scotland. Blythswood and Mission East were working together at the time and set up an office in Tirana during the Kosovo crisis. I was the person on the ground who could help find warehouses and things like that. Then, when they moved to the South East to start a camp for the people, they left me to look after the warehouses. We connected with the local government offices and they showed us the people and places that were most in need so that we could distribute food and other stuff to them. That is how we started.

Then one day the people from Kosovo just left because things had improved in their homeland and they were allowed to go. We had so much stuff and we didn't know where to take it. At the time I happened to be in London for a conference. James Campbell, the Chief Executive of Blythswood, was there and I asked him if I could come and visit Blythswood. So in 1999 I had my first visit to beautiful Scotland. While I was there, Blythswood agreed to support me in my work for fourteen months, and they have supported us ever since. That's why we've been able to help so many poor families in Albania with food and clothing and other things they need.

Children's work

At Christmas 1993, we began to publish the first children's magazine in Albania. About 30 per cent of this magazine was taken straight from the Bible. Back then even the Minister of Education was happy for it to be used in schools. Perhaps because there are so many religions now, religion is not allowed in our schools today, but we used the opportunity to teach children while we had it.

Three years later we started Bible clubs for kids in different churches, two in Tirana and three out of the city. They were called Miracles Clubs after the magazine. We trained leaders in their churches and we visited them ourselves. Our special visit of the year is when we deliver Christmas shoeboxes. We don't only take them to the kids but, since 1999, we have taken them to people of all ages.

Bathore

Most of our work is now in Bathore, which has a population of over 33,000. The people are mainly from a Muslim background. They came from the mountainous north eastern part of Albania where life is very rough and hard. After the country opened up they moved to Tirana but, of course, they couldn't afford to buy houses. So they occupied land without permission and built huts to live in. Since then Bathore has become a priority in our work because there was, and still is, so much need. The need is not only for food and clothes but also for the Word of God.

We started literacy classes in Bathore in 2002 and used booklets especially prepared for that purpose. The two booklets are based on the Bible and teach Albanian at the same time. This was done in cooperation with Literacy Ministries in USA. There was then a great thirst for literacy and for God. In our first groups we had 240 young women coming and wondered what to do for them after the programme was completed. Eurovangelism in Bristol offered us the Alpha course and came to Albania to train course leaders. Because there was such a demand we decided to rent a building and they began to come to our meetings. The women called the building Hope Centre. They said that when they came they went home filled with hope. That's why they chose the name Hope Centre.

Problems

There is a lot of unemployment in Bathore. Some men have permanent jobs and some work on a day-to-day basis, just picking up work when it is around. Most women do not work. In general they have big families and the kids need books to go to school. We have helped, but it doesn't matter how much we give, there is always more need. In our work in that area we try to target young people. If you get the youth, we think, you get the mothers. One problem is that boys there seem to think that they can just order their mothers around. There is that kind of mind-set. So we try to teach about relationships in the family, about husband / wife relationships and parent / child relationships too.

One problem is that all the houses are very close to one another and everyone hears everything. That is not healthy. It is hard for people to break away from their old ways of living and thinking, even for boys to change their way of thinking about their mothers. We have seen some women become

Christians. Husbands usually do not even go to meetings. They are away at work all day and that keeps them from their families and their problems. Also some of the men are very stubborn. Well, we're patient. God has given us patience and we do not surrender. We do not give up. It may take longer. We will keep praying and doing what the Lord shows us he wants us to do.

Vasile Pop

5

A bed and a table – the story of Vasile Pop and the Elpis Foundation, Romania

❖❖❖

My grandfather was the first Christian believer in the village of Capalna near Dej in Romania and I grew up in a Christian home. He was in the army about 1920. Grandpa met some families in Western Romania who gathered together to read a book, the Bible. Being in the army, he was not allowed to have anything to do with Christianity. So when he came back home he sold a cow to buy himself a Bible. After Grandpa understood the Bible, his desire was to have a discussion in front of the people with the Orthodox priest. At that time the Orthodox priest was not able to respond to his questions.

God worked in Grandpa's heart and he decided to follow the Word of God in a very practical way. He was the first evangelical Christian to be baptised by another brother in the area. And he was the person who put aside a bit of land within his property and built a church. His name was Vasile Pop, the same as me. I am glad to say that my grandpa lived long enough for me to remember him and for him to know that I was a Christian. In communist times I heard two voices speaking inside me. I heard teachers and professors who gave me the atheist message and my grandpa and parents who brought the Word of God to my heart. Although I had not at the time been converted, my school teachers knew me as a Christian because of our family's lifestyle.

Due to distance I had to stay at the high school as a boarder. I remember some mornings before I got out of bed my head teacher came into the dormitory and, when my colleagues left the room, he asked to check my wardrobe to see if I had a Bible. I did have a Bible with me but he never found it. We were not allowed to have Bibles or Christian materials with us in school. By that time I had started to pray and to understand that God existed and was real. Even then I understood that the Bible was right and true and that, if I trusted in God, it would be better for me.

True wisdom

When I went to be a student at university I considered my grandpa wiser than my teachers, who had much higher qualifications, for he was kind and understanding and could explain life. Grandpa was different. While I had doubts, I could see the joy and the goal in my parents' and grandpa's lives. Every time he came to our family, he came just to open the Bible. We would hear Grandpa and Mum discussing the Bible as they tried to find the answers to things. In my heart I wanted to know more about the Bible.

Because I wanted to live up to my family's expectations I decided to be baptised. Even though I was baptised I continued to have some battles inside me. I looked around and saw my colleagues living in a worldly way; they seemed happy and I was so tired by my battles. Also I didn't have all the benefits that were given to people who declared they were atheists.

Coming to Jesus

In 1981, when I was around twenty years old and a third year student in the technical university of Cluj, I started to preach. But my heart was not right because there were so many problems for those who had the courage to be different from the Communist Party. One night I was in the university canteen. At that time we only had electric light for two hours in the morning and two hours at night. Many times it just went out. As we ate, my friend looked at me and asked what would happen to me if I were to die that night. At that exact moment the light went out and I was standing in front of God. Nobody saw me, but I said to God, 'Lord, I am here and my life belongs to you. From this moment I want to be sure that you are in my life.' Joy came into my heart and I heard a voice saying, 'You are my child; you are my child.'

A few days later, when I was walking in the streets in Cluj, a voice said to me, 'You are my child, you are not another's.' There were many people round about me. 'And you are my special child,' the voice continued. I started to run on the streets to praise God that I was his child. I had joy. It was a special time and I told God that, if he was accepting me as his child, I would take his Word and apply it in my life. Till then I didn't have any problems with my university studies but a very difficult period was about to begin. Nobody knew what I went through.

Meeting difficulties

I was studying engineering and, when it came to the first exam after I became a Christian, I prayed, 'Now I am your child, I want to see that you are with me. Being your child, you'll let all people know that I am your child by giving me a good result.' That was the first exam I failed. When I came home I said, 'God, I asked you to work in a special way.' And to this he said, 'This is my way to work. Are you ready to accept my way?' It was very difficult for me to accept, but I said, 'Yes.'

Then there was another difficulty. I was in a research area in the university. The university senate decided that all Christians had to declare their faith. My professor was shocked as he hadn't known I was a Christian. Till then he was very pleased with me and announced that he wanted all his students to be like me. Some Christian students decided to say that they were atheists, even though they intended to be back in church the next Sunday. One friend advised that I should do that too. I told him that I was a Christian and knew what I would do, that he had to decide what he was going to do for himself. It was very difficult. I remember going into church that night; it was the most beautiful evening of my life. My friends, students, brothers and sisters knew what had happened. They waited for me and I felt so much love as they embraced me and prayed with me. I genuinely understood the reality of the family of God. It is a real family.

The God of science

At my last meeting of the university faculty I was asked to decide if I wanted to finish my studies or continue to be a Christian. Then they asked how I could accept such a thing as faith. I told them I was there because they had taught me in this way. They were shocked. 'We taught you to be a Christian?' 'No,' I told them, and then I explained that they had taught me the sciences of mathematics, physics etc. and that I could see God in the sciences. God's hand is in the laws of science because all sciences investigate the system he has made. I did not know what they would do. I prayed, 'Lord, if they put me aside, and I am not allowed to finish university, please help my parents to understand. I just want to stay with you.'

What happened was they gave me some points in my final graduation and God used even that to prepare the next step of my life. It was 1984 and he sent me to Oradea. That's where the government decided I should work. I was warned that, if I stirred up trouble, I'd pay for it all my life. My reply was that I was a Christian and I was ready to stay a Christian. What surprised me when I arrived in Oradea was that the director of the factory came to us and said that he wasn't interested in what we believed, what interested him was the kind of people we were and what we were doing. I think

I received the best position of all my colleagues. It was a very good company that made kitchen equipment.

A bed and a table

Before going to Oradea I prayed that, if God was sending me there, he would provide me with a bed, a table and his help. That would show me that he planned me to be there. When I arrived in Oradea I put my luggage in a locker at the railway station and then went to church. There was a meeting after the service and the pastor announced that people were free to leave between the two. Before I stood up I told God I wanted to know where I was to go. I felt a hand on me and heard someone asking who I was and what I was doing there. If nobody had asked me, I would have been ready to go back to the railway station. But because they asked, I knew God was working. Two days later the pastor of the church, the Second Baptist Church in Oradea, stopped me and asked quite pointedly, 'What are you doing here? Would you like to come and stay with me?'

The pastor was Gheorghita Nicolae and from then on I worked closely with him and with Paul Negrut. I was part of their families. And I was invited into the homes of many families in the church because I was alone. That was such a blessing. Once I started to cry and told God my cup was running over. I prayed, 'It is too much for me. Please do not give so many blessings.' Then I started to think there would probably come a time when there would be a valley and I'd have troubles to go through.

My heart's desire

I went to Oradea when I was twenty-four years old. It was not my desire to have a good position, or to have so many blessings, my desire was to be married and have a family. I was already praying for my wife although I did not know who she would be. For more than ten years I prayed for her and that was a very long and hard time.

Because I lived with pastors the people thought I was a speaker and I was forced to start to do ministry I was not prepared for. Right away I worked in the church and was on the list of people prepared to be involved in different programmes and activities. I became involved in youth work too and also began to read and to prepare myself for the ministry. There were around thirty men there at that time; most of them are pastors today. It was a very good time. That was a special period when God worked in a special way in my life.

Five years after I arrived in Oradea the revolution came. After the revolution Iosif Ton returned from the United States. During the communist period God had sent him abroad to study theology and to translate theological books into Romanian to prepare to start a Christian school when communism would fall, which he was sure it would. He said that the time was short to prepare during communism. When he came back Iosif Ton invited me to talk with him and then offered me the job of Executive Director in the Romanian Missionary Society. I worked with him for some years and then moved to the Emmanuel Institute, today's Emmanuel University, as administrator.

Sorina

Sorina, who became my wife, was a student at Emmanuel Insti-tute. We met in church. Soon after we met I told her I wanted to talk with her about my plan to marry and have a family; that I wanted to discuss marriage. Before meeting me, Sorina had prayed that the first person who came to tell her they wanted to talk about marriage would be the right person for her to marry. In two months we were engaged and then married. It wasn't so much about emotions as about God providing, and knowing that Sorina would be a helper for me in the projects that God would give me. We were the answers to each other's prayers.

Things changed in the church in the 1990s. Before the revolution the enemy was outside the church. After the revo-lution the enemy came inside. We saw the love that our broth-ers and sisters in the West had for us through the things they sent. But many tried to hold on to the goods that came, some-times being resentful because other people were given more. I started to see a group of people that had some advantages that others did not have. We were blessed but we did not always use the blessing in the best way.

A shocking diagnosis

In April 1993 we started to work more closely with Blythswood under Jackie Ross, one of the founders of Blythswood. I met him and we talked about the ministry that Blythswood had in prisons. After that we began working in Oradea prison and also started distributing Christian literature. Although Sorina and I did not know it, God was bringing a big change into our lives. By then we had two daughters, Ada, who was two and a half, and Ema, who was five months old. On 6th August 1996 we discovered that Ada had leukaemia. I remember that midnight. I went out of the house into the yard and started crying and praying. I said, 'God, if you will keep her alive, I'm ready to go as a missionary.' At that moment everything changed for me. Three weeks later we put all our things in a van, drove out of Oradea and headed for Tirgu Mures.

We left Oradea thinking that our little daughter Ada had leukaemia but, in Cluj, we were told that was not what was wrong with her. After three months the doctors said they were sure she had mononucleosa and then the diagnosis changed to toxoplasmosis. These are all blood problems. Eventually, when we'd been in Tirgu Mures for six long months, the doctors said that our girl was well! She was healed. I know that many churches prayed for us and God heard and answered all these prayers. That was nearly twenty years ago.

Our plan was to stay in Tirgu Mures for two years because we received a free apartment for that length of time. We were happy to see what God would call us to do after that. I started working in different small churches that were planted there. Over time I learned that it was better not just to plant one church here and another church there, but to develop a vision for a geographical area.

Strategic thinking

Two years later God took us to Dej where I started thinking about how to develop a strategy to spread the gospel and to be more organised preachers. It came into my mind to start a foundation and I asked if Blythswood would allow me to do more than Christian literature distribution and prison work. I was by that time employed by Blythswood. The response was, 'Sure, we are coming to Romania not just to bring a fish; we want to teach you to catch fish.' After two or three months of prayer I understood that God was calling us to start a foundation. That became the Elpis Foundation.

Today the Elpis Foundation runs a Christian kindergarten in Dej, and we have a social worker who assists elderly people around Dej. We encourage Bible study and we have a ministry to prisoners. In Dobrogea, near the Black Sea, we have a day care centre for street children. This is run by a man who grew up on the streets. God called him and he repented and became a Christian. His desire is to help children who live on the streets because he suffered so much as a boy.

He is also planting a church in Galesu. The congregation, which is in its eighth year, is growing. There are forty-five adults and children come to the church too. New Christians come to be baptised and some of them have married. Through this church, formed with children who grew up on the streets in a very poor area, we are starting to work in a Muslim community fifteen kilometres away from Galesu.

We are also involved in Oltenia where a flood destroyed many houses in 2006. Elpis Foundation, in partnership with the Iris Baptist Church in Cluj, which organized the entire volunteering effort, helped build the first new house in that area after the flood. Since then more than 600 houses have been built in Rastu Nou, about seventy of them under the coordination of the Church in Cluj. The first four houses were built by churches in the Cluj area and the Elpis Foundation sent around sixteen volunteers to work on the others. We are continuing to do spiritual work in that place. A church has been planted and we're planning a second one.

A visionary grandfather

As I think back to my grandfather I see similarities between his life and mine. When he died I said a very short prayer. 'God, you began with him,' I prayed, 'but, Lord, I'm here to replace him.' Grandpa was not a pastor; he was a leader. He was not educated, but he was a visionary person. He was the first Christian in the village and the first person to have a bicycle. My grandfather was the first who had a pump to spray his vegetables with water. He was the first who had handles on his grinding stones in the days before flour was ground with an electric engine. I grew up watching him being first at many things, watching him follow his visions. Most of all, I grew up watching Grandpa put Jesus first in his life.

Levente Horvath

6

Interesting times to be alive' – the story of Levente' Horvath, Romania

◆◆

I was three years old when we had to leave our flat at the theological institute in Cluj, Romania, my father having been forced to retire from being a professor there in 1960. Dad tried to defend some theological students who were accused of taking part in secret activities. Some of those students were put in jail and then my father was punished because of his stand. When he turned sixty he was forced to retire; that was part of his punishment. Dad's first wife died in 1954 and he married my mother two years later. When I was born my father wrote a letter to the leader of the evangelical awakening in Romania. He said that I was a late child and that he was praying that the Lord would give him a few years to bring me up. God heard his prayers; he lived until 1989 and died when I was almost thirty years old.

It was a tough life because my father's pension was halved. That was another part of his punishment for what he had done for the students. And my mother lost her job because she was married to a minister. I became used to poverty from an early age but the great thing is that I never felt it. Dad always offered his tithes to the Lord and used that money to help disabled people and others with problems. He always put aside the Lord's money out of the little we had. I learned that from my father.

Family life

Every day we read a chapter from the Bible and prayed. Dad used to tell us, if you read one chapter a day you will read the whole Bible in exactly three years, three months and three days. He started like that in 1928 and continued till his death. I took this for granted until I went to school when I was seven years old. Then I started to realise that the family lives of my classmates were completely different. When I was in primary school we had Ceausescu's picture and a map of socialist Romania in every classroom. We were told that the Communist Party looked after us and that we were the children of the Party. In secondary school we were taught atheism and Marxism and it was always pushed that it was rubbish to believe in God. I was forced to think through the issues and nobody could help me there. If you are taught one thing at home and the opposite at school, after a while you get into a kind of schizophrenic situation and you start to doubt.

I remember when I was age ten or eleven I was first in the class. The school's closing ceremony was on a Sunday morning and my father did not let me go. We were almost threatened to make us attend. Part of me said, 'Yeah, it's not correct.

We should go to church.' The other part of me felt ashamed. Scripture challenges us that, if we are ashamed of the Son of Man in front of men, Jesus will deny us in front of God. I still remember how I wrestled with that as a child. It was difficult. And, of course, my faith was not yet real personal faith.

Dark years

When I was thirteen years old I was so restless to find the meaning of life. I loved my parents but I had to find answers for myself. If God doesn't exist, I asked myself, what is life all about? I decided not to stay a Marxist even though most of my classmates were so brainwashed that they embraced Marxism. Instead, I started to search for other philosophies. Existentialism was in fashion at that time but only selections from books about it were available, not enough to help me.

I remember having long debates about the meaning of life with my friends. Looking back I am so grateful to God because today I can understand most of the atheists' arguments because I have argued them myself. Also I was a teenager suffering from depression, even sometimes feeling suicidal. 'If God does not exist, life doesn't have a meaning,' I decided. 'If I don't find a meaning for my life, why should I suffer any more?' The most rational decision was to end my life. Then, after three years of desperate searching, somehow God found me.

I met three young folk a bit older than me. I was 16 by that time and they were eighteen or nineteen. One of them lived in Budapest and came to Romania. He was a kind of hippy. You know, in Eastern Europe, beyond the Iron Curtain, some young folks tried to imitate the western movements. He looked like one of them; he had long hair and played the guitar. Of course, in Romania the police would seize people like that and cut their hair but for some reason in Hungary that didn't happen.

'Argue with God'

My new friends asked my father if they could come every week to meet him and learn from him. He taught them the Bible and evangelized them. After six months the secret police caught my long-haired friend on the street, cut his hair and put him in jail because he was considered a rebel against the regime. I also met similar guys who came from Budapest. One of them had been a leader in the young communist movement before he had a sudden conversion. He and his friends came to Romania for three days and I invited all my other friends to meet them. I grew very excited about their stories but I launched an attack, trying to argue with them. 'They said, we don't argue. Argue with God.'

These guys just told their testimonies. On the third night, after a long struggle, I fell on my knees and said, 'Lord, if you don't exist, I'm talking to the walls. But if you do, please save me, if I'm lost.' And that's how it all started. I walked home in the early morning and my father was still awake when I opened the door and stepped inside. He knew that something had happened and I said, 'Daddy, I've become a Christian.' I'll never forget the way he cried and embraced me. He said, 'My son, I have prayed for this every day.' So that was the beginning. I was still at school when I became a Christian and often it was hard. Quite a few times secret police officers came to the school and I was called into the head teacher's office.

No other choice

Immediately I became a Christian, I knew God wanted me to be a pastor, despite the risk of ending up in prison. When I was a seminary student, I was sometimes taken to the secret police building. That was quite frightening. I was led along corridors and heard, from different rooms, a terrible cry, probably torturing, or maybe it was just a recording played to frighten me. I never knew. Years later I saw a German film, *Das Leben der Anderen* (The Lives of Others). It's about the East German Stasi. Everything in it reminded me of Romania. It was chilling. But I knew that when these things happened to me I also experienced the presence of the Lord. That was amazing because by nature I am a coward; I'm full of fears. The Holy Spirit gave me words when I had to speak. Somehow I had peace as I started to talk. We used to tell our atheist friends, 'We don't believe in God; we know he exists. We don't need to believe it.' I could almost touch God's presence when I went through these experiences.

I studied at seminary for four years. One day we arrived at the Bible passage about giving to Caesar what is Caesar's and to God what belongs to God. Of course, that was a Bible verse that secret service officers and Communist Party leaders quoted, saying that we had to obey and submit to the communists, that the Bible told Christians to do that. The professor didn't say exactly that. It was left that sometimes you need to obey the authorities. I couldn't keep my mouth shut and disagreed with the professor's interpretation of the passage. He went red and didn't say a single word. Next day a secret police officer came to the seminary to interrogate me. The professor I was with when the secretary came looking for me wouldn't let me go until the class was over. That was just one tiny act of resistance but it was significant. I was so grateful to that professor although I knew that at break I would be interrogated. He wanted to protect the students.

When I was going out with my future wife, I asked if she would marry me. After Maria said that amazing word of confirmation, I paused a little bit and said, 'I'm so glad, but I've got to ask you another question. Will you marry me even if, let's say four or five years after we are married and maybe we have children, I am put in jail? Will you still marry me?' She paused for a while and bowed her head. I'm sure she was praying. That was a big challenge. She could not give an easy answer. And then she said quietly, 'Yes, I have no other choice.'

Ministry in Tirgu Mures

I was ordained in Tirgu Mures and served the church there from 1984 until 1989. Maria and I were married in 1986. In every one of those years the secret police tried to remove me. I think I had been a pastor for about a year when I first met Jackie Ross. He parked his western car outside our home because someone had suggested to him that he come to see me. His car stood out. He said, 'Hello' and I replied, 'Ok, we will talk, but please take your car a few streets away and walk back.' It was never a good idea for a Christian to draw attention to himself; it was never a good idea for anyone to draw attention to himself! Jackie was a bit surprised but he was ok. I did not realise that we were so much under surveillance that his visit would already have been noted.

People flooded to church at that time but the same kind of thirst has never occurred again. Most were quite disappointed with the regime, quite fatigued. There were so many young people coming to church that we had to arrange different groups on different nights of the week because we couldn't fit everyone in. Hundreds of youths came, many of them medical students, and they asked if I could explain my views on abortion. I knew that the regime was anti-abortion and thought I could speak freely as I was agreeing with them. When I had explained the Bible's teaching I gave the young people the opportunity to debate the subject. After a few weeks their number dropped down to forty and that was puzzling.

The following week I asked one of the medical students if the others had stopped coming because I didn't speak well enough. He told me that what I said was good, but that the day after I spoke about abortion the secret police flooded the university. They went into each class and warned the students that, if they wanted a career as a doctor, they should never again go to that young minister, that if they ever turned up in my church again they would be put out of the university without warning. 'Why have you come?' I asked him. 'We need this teaching,' he told me. He and some others put their future careers at risk. They weren't all Christians then but they felt they should come. It was an amazing time. I really loved those times. It was crazy; it was hard. There were dark times, the darkest days of the dictatorship, and yet you could experience such things. It was absurd. I was saying the same as Ceausescu with regard to abortion and still I was being persecuted.

Free, not bitter

We were in Tirgu Mures till 1989. Then I became the pastor of a small congregation in a village nearby called Istihaza, close to Ozd. Maria and I had to tell each other, 'Let's look at this community as if we are in a mission, as though they are pagans.' That was because there were so many bad things going on and people would not attend the church. Many years later, when I was able to see my secret files, I found that two of my church elders were informers who informed about me. God was generous to us because we decided to serve them without expecting anything in return. That gave us a freedom. Otherwise we would have become bitter and wondered if it was worthwhile.

My wife and I were in Istihaza when the revolution started. I've been told that it was good I wasn't in Tirgu Mures because most of the ministers and priests were put in front of the crowd and shootings took place. They could have killed me. Later somebody saw me on the black list when they threw all the papers out of the secret police's building. That person told me, 'It's good that God protected you.' Those were interesting times to be alive.

Many new beginnings

After the revolution the first thing that we set up with my friend András Visky was called Koinonia. It was a publishing house for good Christian literature as we wanted to fill up the void created by the fall of Marxism. We thought that the best thing to do was to set up a publishing house to publish good books, good apologetic books, and reach out with them. The years after the revolution were used for starting up things, things that couldn't possibly have been done before that.

We also created a journal that was a kind of mission to families and we tried to spread the good news through that. Then we thought that, to be strategic about the future, we needed to reach the young folk. That's how the Genesius Association was set up. Some years later we split Koinonia Publishing and Genesius Association into two organisations. I was one of the founders of both. Then in 1993 work with addicts was begun and three years later we registered it as Bonus Pastor Foundation. I don't like to say 'foundation' because in Britain that has a totally different connotation. In the UK, if someone has a legacy and a lot of money, it can be put toward a foundation, but in Romania you could set up a foundation by that time without any money.

There were several other things I was involved in, like founding Blythswood Romania. I was also focussing on the mission-mindedness of my denomination. Till then we had been so insular, people who had to be helped but never considered Jesus' great commission in Matthew 28. 'Then Jesus came to them and said, "All authority in heaven and on earth has been given to me. Therefore go and make disciples of all nations, baptizing them in the name of the Father and of the Son and of the Holy Spirit, and teaching them to obey everything I have commanded you. And surely I am with you always, to the very end of the age".' That's why I started a missionary Bible school to train missionaries for work at home and abroad; it is called the Trans-Silvanus Institute.

Great God, weak man

God has guided us through many changes and over many years, and he has guided us despite my foolishness. Sometimes I went sideways and I regret that now. At other times I wanted to do too much and confused the calling of God with needs I observed. It's very tempting, when you see needs occurring here or there, whether spiritual or material, and you want to help, you want to practise genuine love and compassion. It can be very hard to resist the temptation to do what is good rather than waiting for God to show what is best. I often made mistakes.

I'm grateful for the fact that at such times the Lord would discipline me and remind me that, left to myself, I am just Levente, that I can be completely crazy. He had to show me the danger that I could take disastrous steps. And God had often to remind me that I needed other members of the same body, his body. I needed to act always in consensus with other Christians. Of course, that went against my pride. It went against the way I tend to think that I'm somebody when I'm nobody. We all have this hidden agenda; we all like to be flattered and that's very tricky, very dangerous. I think that God surrounded me with the right people to keep me, by his grace, in a good school of life. How disastrous I would have been without wise Christian brothers and sisters around me.

I feel that my job now is to safeguard the fellowship principle among Christians and this goes beyond my own organisations. I feel called (maybe that's a strong word, but I think it is true) to guard against going astray, to safeguard the biblical example of practising fellowship, even between the east and the west. When people used to ask if we had any needs, I always replied that the biggest need we had was of prayer. Some would reply, 'Yeah, yeah, yeah, but …' And I would say, 'No, nothing else, just your prayers.'

The body of Christ

In the Bible there is a balance between giving and receiving. Paul told new believers that the poor Christians of Jerusalem were giving others the spiritual good of the gospel and that they, in turn, should give material goods to them. It's not that they were poor and you were rich. They were poor in material things but you were rich and they needed your abundancy and you needed their abundancy. There must be a balance in the body of Christ.

What I really liked with Blythswood was that there was this courage of going, sharing, maybe learning, maybe making mistakes but learning from the mistakes. And those who worked, and still work, with Blythswood are sensitive, right back to when Jackie came all those years ago. They asked what would help rather than imposing on us what they thought would help. For me, now, I feel I have to safeguard how relationships are acted out in the body of Christ. As a pastor I have this kind of calling. Of course, I am not here to fix everything, but to remind individual Christians and churches that we are the body of Christ, and that there must be a balance in his body here on earth.

Giving is a grace given to the giver

I often think that when Jesus asked the Samaritan woman to give him water he, by asking, gave, and the woman, by giving, received. This is true gospel reciprocity. You can both give and receive joyfully and that reciprocity makes true brotherly love possible. It is a familial, filial and godly 'kinship' love within the members of the same body of Christ. Why am I insisting that not just giving but also receiving a gift can become genuine love? I can accept your gift freely rejoicing and, by that acceptance, I can give you my love. By accepting I can treasure the giver. This demands reciprocity on both sides.

With Blythswood people I could talk through situations where helping could hurt, and also where not accepting could also hurt. When Jesus, after his resurrection, invited his disciples to have breakfast with him, providing them with fish he had prepared on the shore, he also asked them to add some of the fish they had caught. But who caused them to catch fish that morning? It was Jesus! You see, Jesus handled them with tactful love which was ready, not just to give, but to receive as well. He kept the balance and kindness of reciprocity. And he protected the dignity of those at the 'receiving end.'

My long journey with Blythswood brothers and sisters over the years has taught me how we can protect both the dignity of the giver and of the receiver in Christ. It has also taught me that giving is not a merit of the giver, but is grace for the giver, as much as it is a privilege for the receiver to accept and value what is given. In that way brotherly relationships become real. As Paul stated: 'And now, brothers, we want you to know about the grace that God has given the Macedonian churches. Out of the most severe trial, their overflowing joy and their extreme poverty welled up in rich generosity' (2 Cor. 8:1-2). In other words, an awesome grace of God was given to the Macedonians and that resulted in their wealth of generosity and in their joyful and free giving.

Oana Ciucure

7

My memory of living in a car – the story of Oana Ciucure and Potter's House, Romania

Everyone has heard of the Romanian Revolution that happened in December 1989. When the trouble started I was in fourth year at university studying medicine in Timisoara. I remember that Saturday night being at a birthday party on the university campus. On the way home I heard that there were many fires burning in the town. There were no phones and this news was not on TV; it was all mouth to mouth. It was a very, very sad night.

Next morning I went to the city with some other students to see what had happened. When we saw the police and army around important buildings we joked with them, asking why they were there and saying we hoped they wouldn't shoot us. They told us to leave because they had an order to shoot us. We went to the top floor of a hotel to see what had happened. From there we saw tanks and then the first shooting began. The army began shooting.

I stayed that whole night in the hospital and saw people who had been shot coming in. We cut off their clothes, cleaned their wounds and put on bandages. At midnight some people wearing army uniforms arrived and told us that terrorists had come to Romania and that the army was protecting us. They left with our names and the hospital registers. From then on we hid in different places in the hospital.

At that time a pastor who is now in heaven, Pastor Dugulesku, prayed the first 'Our Father' on the balcony of the opera house in Timisoara. The big desire then was that Bucharest would stand with us against communism and that happened on 21st December. From that day we knew that communism had begun to fall.

Then and now

I was not a Christian then having grown up in a non-Christian family. I didn't know anything about Jesus although I knew there was a God because I had a grandfather who taught me the 'Our Father' prayer. He was my father's father and he was a cantor (he led the singing) in an Orthodox church. From about ten years old and onwards I remember struggling to understand what the goal of my life was. My father was a mayor and a member of the Communist Party. His goal in life was to rise socially and do something good.

In communist times people were normally very poor but, because my father was a communist and a mayor, we could have things other people could not. I remember being in very long queues to get chocolate. We would rise at 4 am to go for milk and there would already be a big queue when we got there. No-one would break the queue because there was fear that somebody could see or hear you. I grew up with fear.

At home we were told that we had to be careful because microphones could be anywhere. People lived in a state of constant fear. I can tell you that even as a Christian that's something that still attacks me today – fear.

When I was twelve years old my father took me from the village and put me in a school in the city. In those times villagers didn't have much chance to leave their village because the difference between villages and cities was so great. My father, with his influence, found a way to move me to a city school. It was very hard because I was put in a family I didn't know. I had to eat when I was told, to do what I was told. That left me with another fear, the fear of hunger. I still sometimes have it when the fridge is empty.

'Our Father'

Always before going to bed I prayed the 'Our Father' prayer as my father's father taught me. And, if I didn't pray, I wouldn't sleep. I went on vacation with my grandfather in the summers. He always took me to church on Sundays and I sat beside him when he sang.

I said the 'Our Father' prayer but didn't know the meaning of it and didn't think of the words. Also when I had an exam I went into the Orthodox church where there was a saint, Saint Anton, who was a miracle maker. I thought that, if I took his books and touched his coffin, I would be helped. Although I wasn't an atheist I didn't know that God has a Son who can give us salvation.

A clever rebel and a smart father

I loved physics and was in third position in the whole of Romania in 6th and 7th grade in physics competitions. It was my desire to study physics. My father tried to encourage me to do medicine but I had developed a little rebellion towards him because he would push me to do things without explaining them to me. I made mistakes with that rebellion because some of his advice was good. One of the things I rebelled against was his idea of studying medicine.

My father was smarter than me. He made an arrangement to take me to Tirgu Mures to meet a medical student and to see the university. They took me to classes and I remember us going into the mortuary where the students were dissecting, and I loved it! That was a turning point and I decided I would do medicine which is why I was in Timisoara at the time of the revolution in 1989.

Student life

Besides being a student I worked as a nurse to support myself. After that I did a one year internship and then entered residency. My first residency was in pulmonology for two years. I finished medical university in 1992 after six years and then worked as a resident doctor and also taught in the nursing school to earn enough to live.

In 1995 I went to the United States to a conference. While I was there I decided to contact someone I knew and we visited places together. When my money ran out I asked her to help me find a job. At that time she still hadn't passed her exams to become a doctor in the United States and she was working with old people, cleaning and doing things like that.

The promised land!

Coming from my background I felt that the US was the promised land! I thought I could work there for a few months and make money. Eventually I found a weekend job working in a nursing home owned by Romanians. When I was given $100 for working two days, I said, 'Wow, that's my salary for two months at home!'

A few days later the woman who worked there on weekdays left the nursing home and they hired me in her place. I extended my visa for six months and stayed in the home. The people loved me and began teaching me English. That couple were Christians and they went to a Baptist church. I remember seeing them on Sundays going to church together with their child nicely dressed and I just loved that. My need of love and seeing a happy family touched me. I asked them how they kept their relationship right. You see, while I was a student I had a broken heart story so I didn't believe that there are men that can be honest and loving and so on. When I saw that couple I really loved what I saw. Even today that motivates me in how I am in my relationship with my husband.

Who is Jesus?

One day I asked them how they could love each other and be so nice with each other. The husband told me, 'It's not us. We are just normal people. It's Jesus.' And I said, 'Who is Jesus?' That was the beginning. He began telling me who Jesus is although it didn't make much sense to me. He also introduced me to the notion of sin and told me that sinners go to hell. I didn't see myself as a sinner because I was brought up to be a good person, helping others, helping colleagues, respecting my parents, respecting work and so on. We had these values.

I began reading the gospels but didn't understand anything. After reading the Bible I remember calling this man saying that I didn't know what it was about. He told me to pray three times a day and read the Bible three times a day. I did exactly what I was told. As I saw how they prayed, I tried to do the same. To me their praying seemed very aggressive. After I was invited to their prayer group where they prayed loudly standing up, I confronted them. I said, 'You're praying just for me to see you.' I was critical, but open and very honest with everything. The man was kind with me. He told me that I needed to show more determination and to keep reading the Bible. That was in 1995.

Back in Romania

I was there for six months and then came back to Romania and used my money to buy an apartment. When I was in the US I applied for a scholarship. After eight months in Romania I received an answer and was accepted. Then I went back to the United States but this time I went to Rochester, New York. I questioned why there are so many religions when there is only one God and became really determined to find out the truth because I was afraid of hell. I met Jesus, not because of his goodness or because I realised how good he was to me; I was looking and searching because of my fear of hell.

A wrong turning

During my eight months in Romania I went to the Orthodox Church, a Pentecostal church, a Seventh Day Adventist church and to the Jehovah Witnesses too. I was in all of them at the same time. When I went back to the US I became very active in the Jehovah's Witnesses and asked for baptism. They wanted to know if I celebrated Christmas, and I said that I did. Then they asked if I celebrated my birthday, and I told them I did. The third thing they wanted to know was whether I would do blood transfusions. I replied that I would because I was a doctor and I believed I could do transfusions. The elders told me that wasn't allowed. After that interview they refused me, telling me I needed to study the Watchtower more until I clarified these subjects. I was broken hearted that day.

Back on the right road

Just then I heard of a Romanian girl who went to West Side Baptist Church in Rochester (now Journey Church) and I went with her. When I felt the peace there I just burst into tears and said, 'This is my place.' It was so overwhelming. I didn't know that was the Holy Spirit. Right away I understood that God is the Father and, if I believed in Jesus his Son, I'd be saved. All that knowledge came to my heart, a totally broken heart. I understood Jesus saved me. He forgave my sins and made me his child. Immediately I joined every prayer group and every Bible study possible. I spent most of my time working in a hospital. Life was church, hospital, church. That was all; there was nothing else.

I found a wonderful fellowship group and a prayer and Bible study group but I couldn't find a ministry. Later on in my prayer group I heard that the church had a place that ministered to downtown children and they needed help. It was called Rochester Family Mission. I went there but, when I saw the people were black, I didn't want to help. In my heart I felt resentment toward gipsies that came from my childhood in Romania. That was a communist way of thinking. I went to the pastor a little fearfully and said I didn't want to go, but was told to apply. At the end of my interview they assured me I was exactly the person they needed.

A change of attitude

After a few months in the church I started working with the children. As I had never worked with children before I didn't know how to do it when I began helping in their Wednesday programme. Eventually the hospital fitted into the programme. They agreed that I could work extra hours on other days and on Wednesdays I was free for Rochester Family Mission.

As I spent more time in the Word of God and going to church I began seeing inside myself, seeing what I hadn't seen before. I called myself a good person but, when I started studying the Bible in depth, I realised what I was really like. When we call ourselves good we are using human standards and not comparing ourselves against the Bible's standards. But when we start reading the Bible and learn God's standards we see how bad we are. I saw that I didn't love these people, that I was judging them and criticising them. These are things that God doesn't love and he opened my eyes to see that.

I began loving these children and I grew up with them as a Christian. While we developed the club I did gymnastics with them and ate breakfast and lunch with them, sometimes feeding them. As well as that I helped with their maths and told them Bible stories. As I did every single little thing with them, I began loving the children. The wall between me and them broke and it was God who broke it down.

Memories of a car

Back in Timisoara in the winter of 1998 I began searching for a church and found one. I went with a group of students from the church to an orphanage because I missed the children. Then I joined another group of students helping street people. There were fourteen places where street children lived. They lived in sewers and in basements of buildings. I began to visit them there. We would take food and pray and talk with them. Somehow I felt that I went to the hospital where people were not welcoming and then I went to see these children who were so loving and so caring and so welcoming.

Until God guided me to my friends Bob and Shelley King in the United States I didn't have a place to stay and slept in a car for three nights. I will never forget that. My memory of living in a car came back and I began to empathise with the children. At first I befriended twelve boys and girls who lived in a sewer. It was amazing watching them. When I went in the sewer I washed their hair and cleaned them from lice. Despite all these things I never, ever suffered from any of their health problems.

Fire!

I tried to get the children to go to church but they didn't want to because they feared being criticised. Then a terrible thing happened. A candle started a fire in the sewer. All the pillows, all the blankets we had given them were burned. The children could easily have died because of the smoke. I was upset because everything we had collected was burnt but much more upset about what could have happened to them. After that I told the girls and boys about God and the fact that they could die and where they'd go if they died. All twelve of them started going to church.

In 1999 my church leaders, in Emmanuel Baptist Church number 3, announced that they wanted to build an orphanage with me as the director. The orphanage was built for the street children. When we were building it many people from other places came to help and they all joined me on the street.

I didn't only go to these boys and girls. Two or three evenings a week I went to children in different parts of the city to feed them. Because many people from my church joined me as volunteers I was never alone. Beside the north train station in Timisoara there were over 150 people living on the streets. We had a rule that they'd get no food if they were on drugs or drunk. I want to say here that I had a prayer group – with twelve girl members – and we gathered to pray once a week.

A change of direction

At the beginning of 2000 it was announced that the orphanage would no longer be for street children; they were too dirty and too miserable. I was very, very upset because the money was being raised for the work using pictures of street children. At that moment I felt used. That work did stop and the donated money was used to begin a new work, the kind of work for which it was actually given.

At first we had street children staying where we worked before. Then the Chosen Romania Foundation was started. Its first programme was Potter's House, a residential program for street boys. That work went on for seven years. When we entered the EU we were told we had to integrate children into families. The time came when we were left with only two boys in our residential care. Then, after much prayer, we decided not to keep the residence open for just two boys, and we would not take on more children as there were two centres in Timisoara which were not full. My husband Nellu and I took one boy called Adi to live with us. The second boy went to another centre.

Complex problems

After that we began a day programme for children who were also from the street but they were called day street children. Many children were sent by their families to beg. They had to get a certain amount of money every day and were not allowed to go home until they had begged enough. These were the street children we took into our day centre. There we tried to integrate them into schools and prevent them from becoming on the streets permanently. The problem was their parents. If we took the children in to help them, they weren't able to beg. Families really needed that money so, when we stopped the children begging, we had to help support their families instead.

Now, praise the Lord, we have a bigger building and we have a large day care programme, not only an after school programme. Potter's House is a place where a fire of enthusiasm goes all the time toward God, a fire of praise, a fire of prayer. It is also a place of evangelism. Our desire in this ministry is to evangelise, to tell children that Jesus is the one and only Saviour, the one and only way to heaven.

Why teach a child? When we teach a child the way he should go, we pray that he will remember it all his life. As well as coming here and doing their homework, the children learn about Jesus and we try to tell their parents the good news too. We keep these children until they become teenagers or adults.

Normal people

My parents were happy that I came back from the States. To start with they were really against the work with street children but it was through that work they met Christians for the first time. They saw doctors, nurses and the pastor all together in a circle, holding hands and praying. Mum said, 'You are normal people like us.' I said, 'Yes, Mum, but we want to share with others, to do good, to pray. That's all we want to do.' My parents accept our work now. I think they see God's miracles in our lives but they are not able to make the big step to faith.

Not I, but Christ

One verse that is very important to us is, 'I can do everything through him (Christ) who gives me strength' (Phil. 4:13). I learned that I do not have to depend on what I can do but rather give myself into the hand of God. Galatians 2:10 is also special. 'I have been crucified with Christ and I no longer live, but Christ lives in me.' Those verses keep me believing that, now that I am a child of God, I am a new person and, if he calls me to do something, even though I don't have the resources, it can be done. It's not me; it's Christ that lives in me.

God's name is on this house

I remember Finlay Mackenzie saying that Blythswood would send us some tents as we had no money for our summer camps that year but knew eighty children planned to come. The camp was at the end of June. A week before that, a Blythswood lorry came and filled the yard with dishes and mattresses, with blankets and tents. It was absolutely over-whelming. Before that we had different friends telling us they could give us tents for two people. We began taking them but we had eighty children and told the Lord we wanted places for at least one hundred people.

In our meetings we kept saying that the tents would come. Then I would go to the Lord and say, 'Lord, don't you see the time is coming close?' And the week before camp we had everything. That's what we see here in Potter's House. It's overwhelming. We built this building with God's resources. His name is on this house.

We see miracles happening in this place as God works through the project day programme, youth programme, family programme and next step programme. And we continue our medical mission and see children and young people coming along. That is why we praise the Lord; everything is his work. With God you can do great things. For Nellu and me Potter's House is our ministry, the place we minister. We don't work here. Nellu works as a teacher and I work as a doctor but this is where we minister together and for Jesus.

Lidia Micula

8

Trust and healing – the story of Lidia Micula and Fundatia Crestina Elim, Romania

My husband Dan and I were brought up in the same church in a village in Beznea in Romania which is about sixty kilometres away from Oradea. As my parents were believers, I was raised in a Christian home along with my two older sisters. My dad was a blacksmith. He worked in a factory but he also had a little workshop at home where he made things like gates.

Our church was in the next village and we walked there twice nearly every Sunday. Dad was an elder and he sometimes preached. Our congregation was a good size, with about 150 people attending services. There were lots of children and plenty of groups to belong to: a choir, a children's choir, a youth choir and an orchestra. So there was plenty to do, plenty to keep us busy. That gave me a very strong sense of belonging.

A surprise for an angry woman

I remember a situation in my primary school when I was about twelve years old. A teacher, who came from the south of the country, was really angry about faith and believers. She made a fuss about those of us who went to church. Although she mocked us in school, I think that our other teachers respected us in a way and didn't bother too much about our beliefs. It seemed to be newcomers who were the ones who mocked us for going to church.

An interesting thing happened relating to that teacher about fifteen years later, long after the revolution. She was still living in our community and a group of Christians went outside her house to sing carols at Christmas. By then we were free to do that sort of thing. Among them were some pupils who had been top of her classes. 'Look at this!' she said, when she saw who was there. 'These were my best pupils.' I wonder if she realised that Christians were among her best pupils when she was teaching us!

Testing times

Oradea is a big enough community that our school didn't know everything about everybody. From time to time teachers asked those who went to church to stand up in front of the class, or they'd make lists of the Christian pupils. By Christian, they didn't mean Orthodox, just evangelicals. When they did that a few others stood as well as me. There would be two or three, perhaps four, evangelicals in the class. Evangelicals were then known as 'repenters'. At that time Romania was 98 per cent Orthodox although it was communist at the same time. It's hard to explain.

You might wonder if we were tempted not to stand, but I don't think we were. Our friends knew who the Christians were and, in a way, it would have been worse not to stand. Maybe it was hard the first few times, but after a while it was like a routine as it happened, I suppose, every month or so.

Move to Oradea

When I was fourteen I went to live with my sister in Oradea because there was no high school near our home. She is nine years older than me and had just graduated from university with a degree in economics. I stayed on with her when I started work in a factory. We didn't choose jobs in Romania then, they were allocated to us. It was a big change going from school to working in a factory.

My sister had a good job but it was not always easy for her. She kept being told, 'You should become a member of the Communist Party if you want to get ahead in your work.' She never did that and therefore prospered more after the revolution than before it.

I am really thankful that I grew up in a Christian family. But, you know, when you become a teenager you question things. I tried doing a few things that I shouldn't have done though I never really thought I wouldn't be a Christian. When I was fifteen, and a pupil at secondary school, I became aware of my own sins and my need to repent. I knew that I had to decide for myself to follow Jesus because I understood that

I wasn't a Christian just because I was born into a Christian family. That was when I came to a personal faith in Jesus.

A real encouragement

Some verses from Hebrews 4 were very special to me at that time. 'Therefore, since we have a great high priest who has gone through the heavens, Jesus the Son of God, let us hold firmly to the faith we profess. For we do not have a high priest who is unable to sympathise with our weaknesses, but we have one who has been tempted in every way, just as we are – yet without sin. Let us then approach the throne of grace with confidence, so that we may receive mercy and find grace to help in our time of need' (Heb. 4:14-16).

That was a very real encouragement to me because I didn't realise up to that point that Jesus was actually tempted, that he really knows what temptation is like. And he really understands. It makes such a difference to think that he's not just up in heaven without understanding of what it is like for us down here on earth. Jesus has lived here and he knows what it's all about, and he knows me too. As well as that, Jesus is the high priest between me and God the Father. I go to God the Father through him.

The revolution

Dan and I knew each other from childhood. Our families were good friends. We were married in 1986 and lived in Oradea. So we were a young couple at the time of the revolution in December 1989 and our first son, Bogdan, was two months old. Although we both worked in Oradea, I wasn't working in December that year as I was at home with our new baby. Dan worked with a telephone company and I was still in the factory.

After the revolution it felt as if something really big had happened. There was a sense of release and freedom for the first time. But, of course, we were not aware how long it would take our society to understand what living in a democracy actually means. I think we had too high hopes at the beginning; we were not very realistic. It is unrealistic to expect a country to change from communism to a democracy in five years. It takes a lot longer than that. In fact, I think it takes a generation to grow up to make that change.

High hopes

I hoped that the revolution would give us higher moral standards. Unfortunately many people who rose to positions of leadership in the country have not had higher moral standards. They have taken leadership as 'their moment' and used it to advance themselves because they knew that they might only have four years in power and then no more. So the moral standards, which had been destroyed by communism, did not get much better when we became a democracy.

Family life has changed. Many of the younger generation enter into marriage with the idea that, if it doesn't work, they can get out of it. As a result there are many more cases of divorce and many more children being brought up in broken families. That's not the way we entered marriage, or our parents.

Fears – then and now

Life is different now. In the communist era everybody had a job; we were forced to have jobs. There was no choice. Because we were allocated jobs, nobody had to worry about finding work. Jobs were not well paid but there was very little to buy anyway. However, there were a large number of other greater worries, like feeling very vulnerable, like knowing you could end up in jail for anything, even if someone told a lie about you. The power of the security police was always a big worry. They could harm your family. We lived our lives under great pressure.

I think that fear was what characterised our totalitarian system. People didn't react to situations, even if they wanted to change them, because of fear that their family would be arrested and imprisoned and tortured. It's the same under every totalitarian system. I've read books about Hitler's Germany and it was just the same there. Today's fears are different. People fear not having jobs, not finding somewhere to live, not being able to provide for their families. These are real fears, especially for the younger generation. But those of us who remember what it was like before the revolution prefer it as it is now, despite the different fears.

Dan

Now I will tell you a little about Dan. When he was in high school in Cluj he went to a Bible study group there. It seems that he had very good mentors in that group. Then, when he came to Oradea, he attended another Bible study. This one was different. It was an underground group that aimed to prepare lay people for leading the church. This was necessary because there were very few pastors. I don't think Dan really thought about becoming a pastor, but he felt the desire to be involved in God's ministry somehow as a lay person. Dan doesn't have a formal theological training. Later a pastor from Marghita asked Dan if it would be possible for us to move there because they had about twelve churches with only one pastor. That is how we came to be here in Marghita.

Looking back I didn't realise exactly what it would mean for us. I was young and we only had one child, Bogdan, who was two years old. Our one room was our bedroom, kitchen, living room, everything. That seems a long time ago! Our second son Ruben was born in 1994. Manuela, our daughter, is the youngest and she was born in 1996.

Help from God's people

In 1991 Philip Ross, son of Jackie Ross one of the founders of Blythswood, came to visit the church in Marghita. I don't know how that came about. Following the revolution there were many needs everywhere and Blythswood became involved in helping the people in our area. Then in 1992 Finlay Mackenzie came with Philip and brought aid. We saw and experienced the love of our brothers and sisters who cared for our needs. Even though it was very challenging travelling to Romania at that time – a lot of waiting at the borders, queuing, paperwork, stamps and rude customs officers – Blythswood people didn't stop coming. Since then, our relationship has turned into friendship and we continue to work together.

About the same time as Philip came, we met some visitors from a church in Sweden. They were very touched to see television programmes about Romanian orphans and wanted to be involved in helping them. Our senior pastor Nelu Cocis knew a Swedish pastor who, together with his wife, risked coming to Romania to preach even before communism fell. As a result a church group from Sweden made a connection with Marghita church. They came to visit a few times a year. Some rented a house and stayed longer, working as volunteers with abandoned babies in the local hospital and in a boarding school in Popesti.

Family life

I very much enjoyed being a young mum and was blessed that I stayed at home and raised my children until Bogdan was ten, Ruben was five and Manuela was three. I was there for them and tried to lay the foundation for a good start in life. I had time to play with them, read to them, ride our bikes and other wonderful things that we shared together. Now they are adults and, when they talk about their childhood, it is always fun. All three are now involved in the church, working with the children and leading the Awana Children's Club and also they are part of the worship team. We are very blessed to see them passionate and involved with the Lord's ministry.

Sometimes they remind me about embarrassing and funny situations, or mistakes that I made as a parent, or pranks they did, some of which I only find out now. For instance, when they were small I had a cassette tape with stories and poems for children and we listened to them together. One poem was called 'A little worm.' It talked about how a small lie, which in the poem was a little worm, brings into a child's heart other bad things that are bigger and bigger and more dangerous animals: an owl, a fox, a wolf, an octopus and so on. I thought it was a very good educational poem. Recently they told me that they were terrified each time they listened to it! My husband said about those times that, 'We didn't have much, but we had what we needed, because the Lord was with us and he overwhelmed us with his care and grace.'

Fundatia Crestina Elim

Because Dan and I knew a little English, and there were very few English speakers, we became involved with our Swedish friends who worked with orphan children. The leaders and the heart of the groups were Lars and Barbro Gustavsson. For a number of years I was a volunteer helper, translator etc.. As we became more involved we wanted to be part of the healing the orphans needed. In 1996 our Swedish friends started what is now known as Fundatia Crestina Elim (Elim Christian Foundation). Three years later, one of them, Iorela, returned home after about seven years. She was the project leader of Casa Alba orphanage. I worked alongside her for one year and then took over her responsibilities. Since then I've worked with FCE.

As my husband and I were helping FCE as volunteers, we knew about their work and their needs. That was why we asked Blythswood to bring the kind of things that would be useful in taking care of the children: food, clothing, toiletries, even furniture. And I must mention the Christmas shoeboxes which are still such a highlight for the children. Blythswood has been a very steady, long-term supporter of the work of FCE. And not just for the Foundation, but for the believers as well.

An answer to prayer

That is how FCE began. Now I will tell you about an answer to prayer. In 1994 my husband started the Baptist church in Popesti. There was just one Christian family attending and a few interested people, around ten altogether, meeting in someone's home. Coming from an Orthodox background, where the church building is very important, local people didn't consider a house as a church and were very shy to attend. My husband prayed for a solution and wanted to buy a building to be used for church meetings. He shared his vision with Finlay Mackenzie, from Blythswood.

On going back home Finlay and his wife, Wendy met an elderly lady in a supermarket. She asked how the trip to Romania had gone. Amongst other things, Finlay told her about Popesti and the need for a place of worship, mentioning that there was a piece of land with an old house on it that had potential to be useful. A few minutes later, the lady came looking for them and told Finlay that she would donate the money to buy the land and property. Isn't that amazing? This is how our Lord works and that lady will have such a wonderful reward in heaven. We succeeded in replacing the old house with a new church. The church in Popesti has grown and we enjoy the Lord's presence each

Sunday. I can't put into words how much we appreciate the work of Blythswood and I'm sure it has blessed millions of people over the years.

University and beyond

After our family grew up I went to Babes-Bolyai University in Cluj-Napoca to study psychology. When I graduated in 2007 I was already working with FCE. A colleague said that it would be good if I would apply for a job in a special needs school that was newly opened in Marghita. It was opened in collaboration with the Foundation and they really wanted it to be different from a normal special needs school. It was influenced by western principles. When I started studying I never thought I would work with children with special needs.

I chose to study psychology because I felt a need to learn more about what happens in children who don't benefit from proper care as babies, to know what goes on in their minds and hearts and how to help them. I was very amazed many times at university when people boasted about new scientific discoveries in psychology when I knew that they were already in the Bible. The first example of that which comes to mind is love. People have done very significant studies about how important it is for a baby to be loved as though that was an interesting and exciting new discovery! And I thought when I heard them, 'Well, the Lord is ahead of us.'

I'm just overwhelmed at how God created us, how the brain functions. Neurochemistry is so absolutely amazing that it actually leads you to worship the Lord. I mean, how does a specific chemical know that it is to be released in the body, at what time and what place? It's amazing!

Special children with special needs

I've been involved with children with special needs for a long time. My first contact was with abandoned children and it would be true to say that almost all of them have special needs. Some of those we worked with were adopted and we don't have contact with them any longer. Many have chosen to come back and see us, even from the United States. We have heard such very good stories of their development and how families have been blessed to have them as well as them being blessed by being brought up in loving families. So, yes, there have been good outcomes with some of the children, but not all. Others will have life-long problems.

One of the things that is present in almost every child who suffered deprivation is a lack of trust. This is again a scientific thing, connected with the early attachment cycle in the child. If he doesn't get that before he is two years old, he will always have problems with trust. Of course human interaction is lacking. If a child lacks trust, he lacks everything.

I've seen some children who don't trust people very well but who have learned to trust God. That becomes such a healing for them. I've also seen a few of them come to church and receive the Lord. They really do have healing and can connect better with people and with the church after that. I think they feel that people can let them down but God can't, and this is such a wonderful thing. Speaking of the human outcomes then, if we look at those who come to church, they are better balanced. They cope better in social settings and are more likely to keep their jobs.

The church family

I think that part of the church's role is to be a family, and a family that welcomes others like these children. In our church there are quite a few young people who come each Sunday, maybe about ten of them. Those who truly want to integrate and go with the church young people, grow and really do belong. They feel that the people in church accept them because we actually do accept them. It's a very good thing for them. I think that the Lord meant the church to be like that, to be a place of healing.

There are no longer orphanages full of abandoned children in Romania. But unfortunately there are still abandoned children, quite a number, but the social system has changed and these boys and girls are not kept in big institutions. They are placed in family homes, which is far better for them.

Do it now!

In our classes we have both children who come from normal families and have learning difficulties (some have both learning difficulties and physical disabilities) and also we have a few that have been abandoned. They also face learning difficulties, severe learning difficulties. I feel very blessed in this school, and in this time in history, because I have freedom to talk about God to the children. It is great to have that freedom but we cannot take it for granted. Now we see in other modern democracies that freedom is gradually being taken away. I realise that and I feel, 'Oh, do it now,' in case the freedom is removed. Children with special needs, who are mentally delayed, can be very straight and sincere and open. They listen when you teach them God's ways. They listen and they believe what you say.

If you could come and see my country, you would see two different things, things that sometimes still surprise me. On one hand it's the malls, the nice shops and also quite a few nice new houses. But on the other hand most of the people struggle to make ends meet, and there are many, many people who still live in real poverty. One reason for the nice houses is that their owners went to work outside the country and sent money back to Romania. If you just look on these streets, you can think this is all a very good country. But I think you should look at other places too where there is still a lot of needy people.

Our Foundation is involved with an after-school programme. Some of the families we go out and visit are doing very badly. Some don't have shelter; some don't have a stove for cooking or heating. It is difficult for families in this situation to get out of it because they don't have education. And as they are too old to go to school, they can't get jobs. Honestly, I don't see a solution to their situation.

Migration

And we have another problem because so many young people leave Romania, at least for a time. Traditionally, when parents become older, their children take over and care for them. Many who are left behind when their children go abroad feel they are not cared for, and it is true that some are not cared for. That means that we need nursing homes for our elderly people but that is such a change of mind-set that it badly affects old parents. They feel abandoned.

Not only that, migration affects churches too. The church's young people leave and you can understand why. Some of our church families left to go to the UK. The interesting thing is that they said they would come back and one couple is actually coming back soon. That is good news for us. Basically they went to the UK for a time to save up to pay their debts and now they are coming home to make their lives here.

Dan and I have stayed in Romania. It is our home and it is where we are able to serve the Lord. We are grateful to Blythswood for supporting the work we do for the Lord and for the children of our country.

Dumitru Sevastian

9

The lost boy – the story of Dumitru Sevastian, Moldova

I was born in the south of Ukraine about forty kilometres from the Moldovan border and I am ethnic Romanian. I grew up in a Romanian village in Ukraine with three brothers, three sisters and me in the middle. Dad was a lorry driver and his usual load was compost. Mum worked on a chicken farm. When Mum was working the older children looked after the younger ones. I went to school when I was six years old.

Mine was a Christian family which was why the atmosphere in our home was good. Our parents' attitude was very positive. They worked hard to have a Christian family but the influence of teachers and all kinds of propaganda was very strong. School teachers had a different attitude to children from Christian homes. At that time parents were not allowed to take children to church. If they did take them, they could be made to pay a fine.

Sometimes teachers even came to church to see who was taking their children to the services. If they found children there, they would sometimes laugh at them when they saw them in school, even in front of other children. The Soviet system looked at evangelicals as inferior people, as if they had mental health problems. Sometimes they'd say that evangelicals were their enemies because they were agents of the United States or followers of capitalism. Despite all of that our parents took us to church with them.

Do this, don't do that

As we were growing up we did not understand Christianity and things weren't really explained to us. We were just told we had to go to church, to pray and we had to do this or not do that. I don't think that many Christian parents then had enough knowledge to explain the faith to their children or answer their questions. If we owned a Bible, we had to read it and we had to avoid serious sins. They didn't talk about living in a relationship with God. Even in church we did not hear talk about things like that. It seemed to be all about keeping laws.

As I grew older I decided, along with some boys from other Christian families, that we would get involved in sport in order to be strong. Partly we thought that other boys would not look down on us if we were stronger than they were. We could even have beaten them in a fight. But that wasn't a solution. Because of all the propaganda they heard the other boys were always telling us that their lifestyle was far better than ours.

I'm not going back

When I was about sixteen years old I told my parents that I wouldn't go to church anymore because I wanted the lifestyle I saw other boys having. My two older brothers made the same decision. The Soviet system tried to make people live according to the Bible but without God. In reality people just lived as they pleased. They laughed at evangelicals. If you were an evangelical Christian, you were punished because you couldn't study at university or have a position in society no matter how clever you were. It was very difficult to grow up in a Christian home knowing how much you could not do and what having faith would cost you.

After leaving school I went to Chisinau to study telecommunications in college. There I had friends from my village and I also made other new friends. Because I was far from home I lived without my parents' guidance and without God's help. I could be happy sometimes, especially when I was doing sport. If anyone invited me to do something, I did not say, 'No,' in case they thought I was afraid. I was strong and I was not afraid. Even when invited to do different bad things, I didn't say, 'No.' The kind of life I was leading led to me committing a crime against another person and I was put in prison for six years.

Prison

While I was in prison I had time to think because I was away from the pressure of propaganda and of friends. It was then that I realised that my family were my friends. They were the ones who stayed close to me and never asked me why I did what I did. Several times my childhood seemed to pass in front of me and also the life I had lived just before I committed my crime. When I compared them I saw that my life in Chisinau had been hopeless, much worse than my childhood. And I could see that my parents' lives had meaning.

I started to think about God and remembered my childhood and going to church. And I remembered my father reading the Bible with us, even if he didn't explain it. He also prayed with us every day. Six months after I went to prison, on 20th December 1987, there was nobody else present, just myself and Jesus, when I repented of my sins. From that time, even though I continued in prison, my life totally changed. Dad taught us all many Bible verses when we were children and I found I could remember them. They were my Bible in those days.

The lost boy

One of the stories I remembered very clearly was the story of the prodigal son and I understood it to be about myself.

Jesus told this story: 'There was a man who had two sons. The younger one said to his father, "Father, give me my share of the estate." So he divided his property between them. Not long after that, the younger son got together all he had, set off for a distant country and there squandered his wealth in wild living. After he had spent everything, there was a severe famine in that whole country, and he began to be in need. So he went and hired himself out to a citizen of that country, who sent him to his fields to feed pigs. He longed to fill his stomach with the pods that the pigs were eating, but no one gave him anything.'

'When he came to his senses, he said, "How many of my father's hired servants have food to spare, and here I am starving to death! I will set out and go back to my father and say to him: Father, I have sinned against heaven and against you. I am no longer worthy to be called your son; make me like one of your hired servants.' So he got up and went to his father.'

'But while he was still a long way off, his father saw him and was filled with compassion for him; he ran to his son, threw his arms around him and kissed him. The son said to him, "Father, I have sinned against heaven and against you. I am no longer worthy to be called your son".'

'But the father said to his servants, "Quick! Bring the best robe and put it on him. Put a ring on his finger and sandals on his feet. Bring the fattened calf and kill it. Let's have a feast and celebrate. For this son of mine was dead and is alive again; he was lost and is found." So they began to celebrate' (Luke 15:11:24).

In prison I was very glad that story was written in my memory from my childhood, that my father had put it there. It was amazing to me that my human father and mother wanted me back despite all I'd done, and even more amazing that Jesus was waiting to accept me when I repented of my sins. That story is my story and the story of everyone who becomes a Christian.

Big changes

I was in prison for another five and a half years after that. From 1990, following the fall of communism, the government permitted evangelical Christians to go into prisons and preach the gospel. I was very happy to meet some of them. Before that, even after I had repented, the prison authorities didn't let me have a Bible. After 1990 I had fellowship with a group of Christians and the pastor from Chisinau Baptist Church. I shared my desire to be baptised and then was baptised in the prison yard. It was the first baptism to be held in that prison.

Other prisoners also came to faith. We made a prayer room and spent time there, praying together, reading the Bible together and explaining it to each other. Every day we had these kinds of meetings. When one prison friend was released he gave me his sister Luba's address. She and I corresponded and eventually she agreed to marry me. We were married in 1991, in prison, and it was the first wedding in the prison. About six months later I was moved to another kind of prison where I had more liberty. Luba moved to that town and we were able to live together. I reported to the prison every day and worked in construction and we could attend church. There were other restrictions, for example, we could not leave the town without permission.

Put God first

The scriptures were very important to me at that time, and still are now, especially the gospels because I love Jesus' life and his attitude toward people. 'But seek first his (God's) kingdom and his righteousness, and all these things will be given to you as well' (Matt. 6:33) meant a lot to me then and has done over the years. Put God first. Put his will first, his plan first and the rest will happen according to his will and will be for the best. That doesn't mean the best in the eyes of the world, but the best God has for you. It's amazing to walk with God, to see how he changes you and sometimes changes others through you. Life hasn't always been easy, but it has been blessed.

During my years in the open prison I started to preach. At that time the first Bible school in Chisinau was opened and I was invited to study there. It was a one year Bible course. An old lady said she would like our family to stay in her home without payment. She was so kind to us. The year that I attended the Bible school was very good because we studied the Bible from eight in the morning till five in the afternoon.

An invitation

After that I received an invitation to continue my studies in St Petersburg Christian University. I asked Luba and a friend to pray about it. We prayed that, if God wanted me to study there, the person who invited me would find some information for me. He went to the university for a few days and, when he contacted me on his return, he said that he had some information for me and would like to meet to talk about my future studies. God was leading us forward.

Towards the end of studying in the Bible school the Director, who was from the United States, asked if we students would agree to have a week of vacation because he and his wife were celebrating twenty-five years of marriage and wanted to go for a short break in the country. My friend Sasha and I had just received a letter inviting us to take the university entrance exams. If it had not been for that wedding anniversary, it would have been impossible to leave the Bible school for a week.

As I had no money to go to St Petersburg, I shared with my colleagues that I had a need and asked them to pray about it, without telling them what the need was. Afterwards, one student said, 'I don't know what need you have, but God wants me to answer your need.' I explained the problem to him and he said that he would bring me $20 the next day.

Sasha and I passed the entrance exams. We were happy. They told us that, as we had been at Bible school, we could start in second year. Then it was explained that we would have to pay $900 per year – $300 for our room and $600 for our studies, and we would also have to pay for our travel, food and everything else we needed. This was said to someone who just that week didn't have $20 for the train fare!

God is not a billionaire

Our feelings were very mixed. There was joy and not discouragement, but sadness too, because we had passed the exams but didn't know if we could become students at the university. I remember the words of the Rector of St Petersburg Christian University, Dr Peter Penner. He said, 'Remember that God is not a billionaire. Everything belongs to him. If he wants you to be here, he'll help you. You'll find all the support you need. Have peace.'

When we returned to Chisinau Sasha and I shared the news with our Director. He congratulated us. That was all; no help. It was the same when we told our pastor. The church couldn't help us. 'But,' he said, 'last Thursday a missionary from the United States asked me to suggest the names of two young people we could send to St Petersburg to study. He said that he would support them and that, after finishing university, they would come back and serve the Lord in Chisinau.' The pastor went on, 'I'll ask him if it was a joke.' It was not a joke and God used that man to send us to the Christian University in St Petersburg to study. That was how God supplied all our needs. Our oldest child was born in Moldova and our other two children were born in St Petersburg.

For the next two and a half years Sasha and I studied at the university. Then we came back to Chisinau and I was sent as a missionary to a church not far from there. The church grew from twenty to forty members in the eight years before we moved back to Chisinau and I became one of the pastors in Bethany Baptist Church.

Join the family

The leadership of the church proposed that Luba and I look after a ten-year-old boy and his sixteen-year-old sister as well as our own three small children. Their mother died very young of cancer and their father died in an accident years earlier. Before their mother died some Christian women visited her and, as far as I know, she received the Lord. She asked these women to look after her children. When the leadership of the church made that suggestion we prayed about it and accepted. For eight years we cared for the brother and sister and still have very good relationships with them.

As well as being a pastor I understood that my calling was to be involved in the Bible college in Chisinau, serving the young people and praying for them. I also continued my studies part time, following two masters' programmes and, in 2012, receiving a Ph.D. from the University of Wales. The college in Chisinau is now a Christian university, the first one in Moldova, and I continue the same ministry in both the church and the university.

Blythswood

During this time I met people from Blythswood. It is amazing how God brought together those who shared the same vision and I am very thankful for this partnership. Blythswood helps people in need. Everyone's greatest need is to know Jesus and together we share the gospel. But at the same time Christians have to show the love which we see in Jesus by helping others.

We believe that Jesus is not only our Saviour but also our Lord, and he's a loving and a good God. If we really have these convictions, we'll try to do the best we can to follow him in the way he looked after people in real need, even when the religious leaders just laughed at him. Over the years we have seen people coming to Christ, especially those we serve. This is not just because they want to receive help but because they see and understand God better through the ministries which we have in our church with disabled people, with old people, with children, with homeless people and with those with other needs.

Victory Day

All kinds of people come under our care. For example, we have a ministry to veterans. For years we organised a meal for them before Victory Day on 9th May. The jackets of the veterans who came were virtually hanging with medals, some on both sides because they fought on one side and then on the other. Many of them had fought at Stalingrad, one of the worst battles in the Second World War. Our church made a very beautiful meal and the tables were overloaded with food. We also made up little parcels for the men and women to take home with them.

If you watched carefully, you'd see the veterans taking a sandwich and putting it into a bag, looking about and taking another little bit of food and putting it into the bag too. These men and women fought hard. Then they lived under communism for many years and had nothing to show for it. At the dinner they were stocking up with food for the next day even though they were being given a gift as they left. The church let the veterans know that Christians cared for them and remembered them.

Now there are fewer veterans and they are in their nineties. Until recently we brought them for a meal, shared the gospel and talked together for a time. Last year our sister Valentino visited them at home instead because most of them just stay in their beds now and cannot go out.

Who is Jesus?

Many Moldovans are nominal Christians. That allows them to consider themselves to be religious and to be materialistic at the same time. They live as they want to live but their lives show that they do not have a real faith in God. People don't talk about Jesus as their Saviour; they talk about laws that God wants them to keep. It's about not committing big sins, big crimes. Most consider that God *has* to accept them rather than God being gracious enough to accept them through the death of Jesus Christ on the cross.

If you ask nominal Christians who Jesus is, most will tell you that he is a good example, not that he died to save sinners. That's why we have to talk to these people, to explain that Christianity is not just about keeping laws. Christianity is about relationship; it's about a living relationship with God through Jesus Christ, his Son and the one and only Saviour.

I am happy to be God's messenger, to serve the people of Moldova and to try to meet their needs with the help of my friends from Blythswood. And I am thankful to Lord for this partnership.

Adrian Popa

10

Get up, little girl – the story of Adrian Popa and Talita Kum, Romania

My parents were both Christians living in Romania, a communist land. By the time I started school I was attending church with my father. In my first or second year at school I was denied the right to wear the red tie as a communist Pioneer and was the only one who didn't have one. Later it was embarrassing to be asked in a class of eight or nine year olds if we believed in God, and to discover that only one other child did. We were asked if we'd seen God and there was a bit of giggling about it.

When we were told to go to school on a Sunday I explained my dad said that I didn't have to attend school activities and projects as we were going to church. They did not do normal school work on Sundays; it was things like planting trees and cleaning parks for two or three hours. I told the teacher that my dad said I wasn't to go and, if she had an issue with it, she should take it up with him. Even then I was learning to defend what I thought.

When I was a boy I knew what I wanted to be when I grew up. I have very clear memories of wanting to be a bus driver. I travelled by bus most of the time and liked the bus drivers. Strangely, I also liked the smell of burned fuel and, I can't believe it now, but I could stay for some time at a bus stop inhaling the aromatic hydro-carburant fumes ... probably petrol!

I didn't like communism. As I was growing up I found communism boring rather than exciting. It was a wooden language that didn't really do anything for me and was never a realistic alternative belief system. The alternatives that might have attracted me were secularism, atheism and nominal Christianity. They were on the table as options.

Community

Growing up in the church gave me a very strong sense of belonging to the Christian community. That didn't make me good and I was quite naughty at times. Occasionally I skipped school and went to a movie but my parents found out about that. To be honest, the things of the world didn't appeal that much to me because I was with Christian friends most of the time after school and on Saturdays and Sundays. I played in an orchestra and in a wind band in church and I started to learn a few instruments. That's the kind of thing that appealed to me. My sense of community, of belonging to believers, was so strong that I was spared most of the troubles that some other children from Christian families went through.

A powerful sermon

When I was fifteen years old a famous evangelical preacher came to Dej. He preached a very powerful and emotional sermon. Most of my friends responded but, although I was touched by the sermon, I felt it was not for me. One day I asked Dad, 'What do my friends have that I don't have? What do they feel that I don't feel?' My dad's answer was very wise. 'It's about looking into your heart and your mind and asking yourself if you trust Christ.' That's when I realised that people's experiences are all different. No two people think and feel exactly the same.

The following year I moved to Jimbolia to live with my grandparents and I attended church in Timisoara. Before long I went to my pastor and said that I was a Christian and wanted to be baptised. I frequently memorised scripture and from a very early age I liked to learn psalms. The people in our congregation often recited poems. I was a little non-conformist and said, 'Well, I know some poems, some great poems,' and I put my name down to recite them. When I stood up I recited the psalms and everyone said, 'But you said you were going to recite poems.' 'These are my poems,' I told them.

A rational thinker

I have never liked the idea of having short Bible verses as favourites, and I've never felt that God has spoken to me through a 'special' verse. You can see that I have not been very romantic in my thinking even though I was brought up in a romantic age and with romantic speech. The sermons I heard as a child were very flowery and emotionally charged. There was a lot of crying and pastors preaching with tears. But I was never taken up by the romantic spirit and was rather dull and boring and just plain rational. Even as a young person I tried to be as cerebral as possible. Looking back, I have not courted experiences. I don't dispute or deny such experiences; they are just not for me.

Of course, being away from my parents meant I had less supervision. Reading Christian books and playing my musical instruments took up much of my time. I also started teaching children in Sunday school and wrote and preached my first sermon by the age of seventeen. Even then I had a taste for theology, especially Christology as I wanted to understand Christ as the revelation of God.

National service

Because I had to do my national service, I knew that whatever work I did after leaving school would be an interim job. We did not have a free choice of jobs; we were told what to do. I was interested in mechanical engineering and metal work at the end of high school and went to work in a factory in Timisoara that built large excavating machines for the mining industry. I worked in the factory for two or three months and then began my national service. That should have lasted fourteen months but was extended to sixteen.

National service is not easy for anyone in any country, whether in conflict or not. Because you are basically being trained to kill they need to toughen you up. Christians doing national service in Romania then had a lot to put up with. Amazingly my very good, neat handwriting protected me. Within a few days of starting my superior noticed my handwriting and I was made secretary to the commander of the unit. From then on I practically didn't know what it was like to be a new conscript.

Found out

We weren't allowed Christian literature but I smuggled in a very, very tiny Gospel of John. It was so small that it was almost impossible to read. I was found out and told to go up with other people who were discovered with Christian literature, or some other such thing, and we were disgraced publicly just to embarrass us. However, the commander bailed me out. In private he asked if I really believed or if I was just going through the motions of being Orthodox. Then he asked if I had any friends abroad, or had any association with any organisations outside the country. I assured him that I did not. As I couldn't speak German or English at the time, he probably believed me. He would have checked me out anyway as background files were kept on everyone. In the end he told me off privately and I got away with it. The commander was in the habit of trusting me because some of the documents I wrote for him were classified.

The second part of my national service was very easy. Because I was a bugler I had a room to myself. As well as playing the bugle I continued to write for the commander and only went to shoot when they had training sessions. I had time to read and probably read half of the library that we had in the unit. That was when I realised that I wanted to study more and become an engineer. I knew I didn't want to go to university; that just wasn't for me. My father was disappointed but I wanted to work with my hands just like him.

After finishing my national service I went back to my former job for two years. I was so busy I didn't have time to prepare for the engineering exam and didn't take it. By the time the exam came round again the following year I was more interested in studying theology. I was by then twenty-three years old, and was being asked to preach more and didn't like to do that without training.

Ritta

Ritta and I met in church. She was converted aged sixteen or seventeen. We knew each other for three years and were married in 1988 when she was nineteen. At the same time as I asked Ritta to marry me I asked the seminary in Bucharest to accept me as a student. I asked two institutions to take me on – sort of! Knowing nothing about the seminary, I didn't even realise that the maximum number of students allowed by the communist regime was four. Even though I'd no influential connections in church or state I was accepted as one of the four. That was a surprise to me. When I went to Bucharest to study Ritta stayed at home and I travelled to see her every two months.

I was at home at the time of the revolution in December 1989 because we'd been sent away early for our holiday. I didn't go out on the streets, just watched television and waited for things to happen. In late autumn we had known about unrest from the news on Radio Europa Libera. I do not think there would have been changes without decades of Free Radio broadcasting balanced news. Although things were obviously happening, I didn't believe for one moment that the Ceausescu regime would collapse.

A different city

When I went back to Bucharest in the new year it was a very different city. There were things that we could do that we weren't allowed to do before. I started to take some extra classes. Along with others I found a teacher and studied with him. A pastor in Bucharest paid for us to do that. I also looked for people who were very good with preaching and expository teaching of scripture. Although the college began to add good English books to the library, I wasn't able to access them as I had no English. Frequently I went to a very fine Christian poet called Ioan Alexandru. I also went to Beniamin Fărăgău in Cluj because he had learned many things from the Navigators that he could pass on to me. Knowing there was much that I didn't know, I did all I could to broaden my perspective.

Even after the revolution I felt that communism was alive and kicking and I never surrendered my anti-communist convictions. Nor did I entertain socialism of the sort associated with President Iliescu and his party. Although they won the next two democratic elections with a large majority of votes, I was always a rebel in that regard.

At the end of my second year at the Baptist seminary, three of us were given the opportunity to study at The Evangelical

Theological College of Wales (now Wales Evangelical School of Theology). We were told we'd learn English there. All three accepted the offer and decided we didn't require an extra year to complete the course, that we'd rather push ourselves and learn English quickly. Two months after arriving in Wales I wrote my first essay in English and was awarded an A. I don't think I deserved it, but it was very encouraging!

Enter Blythswood

For the first year in Wales we were supported by the Romanian Missionary Society and I also had support from a Baptist church in Weymouth for my second year. But I still had two years to go. Philip Ross was in the year below me at college and he had given me some magazines that showed the work Blythswood was doing in Romania. Philip's father, Jackie Ross, was one of the founders of Blythswood. I was very interested in what my he showed me. When Philip heard that I was struggling financially, he said, 'We could ask Blythswood.' Then at the end of term, when I left to go back to Romania for the summer, Philip said, 'Do come back because Blythswood is willing to support you.' When we returned after the summer that's what happened.

Ritta had joined me after one year in college because we were given the use of two rooms in the librarian's house. Then Gilgal Baptist Church in Porthcawl offered us their manse. We lived there for five years until I completed my doctorate. I was invited by the church to consider staying on at the end of my studies but I explained that I wanted to return to Romania.

My reason for returning was one of integrity. The purpose for which I'd been given a visa to stay in the UK no longer stood. I went back home with a view to doing pastoral work.

A difficult time

To start with I contacted the people who had believed in me before I left. First I went to see Paul Negrut in Oradea and told him I had a doctorate in Old Testament studies and a Ph.D. in Hebrew. I offered my services but he didn't take up my offer. I wondered if, at some time in the past, I had given the impression of being more liberal in my theology than I am in fact. Maybe he thought that it was his duty to protect the college in Oradea from anything that didn't sound like Southern Baptist Convention. I definitely didn't!

After that I asked myself whether I had surrendered any of the core evangelical beliefs that I grew up with, that I shared with people in the church. Paul Negrut had the right to say that, if I didn't share the same views as him on some things, I couldn't teach in Oradea. I had to ask myself before God what I had done. My answers were that I had lived for seven years abroad and had gone to a very evangelical, very reformed, very good college. I felt disillusioned, but still justified my opponent. I was taught in school to do that and still do it to this day. When I asked myself, if I were making his argument, would I feel it was right, I knew that I would. If I were him, I would feel justified in deciding, 'I have my interest at stake and I can say no to Adrian. He's young and he could be worse in years to come?' Maybe he was right!

'This is my country'

I came back to Jimbolia and made one more attempt to find a teaching position, thinking that, if Oradea wasn't interested, the seminary in Bucharest might be. So I visited the principal but there was no place for me there either. For a while I wondered about going back to Wales. But then I said, 'Hold on. This is my country. This is where I can make the greatest contribution. I have a vested interest in this country. Things would have to be very, very bad for me to move away again.' After that I served as pastor in a church for two years and was invited by the congregation to become their full-time pastor, but the appointment was never ratified. However, that was an encouraging time as there were about thirty children coming to Sunday school and staying for the church service, and I could see the impact of the preaching. While I was pastor there I taught Romanian and English in a local state secondary school and Ritta was working too.

A bigger problem

Something happened during the time that I was pastor in the church and teacher in the school – God used the school children to open my eyes. To this day I think that the most important time in my career was those two years when I taught in a state school. It was then that I became aware of real poverty. For seven years in Wales I had seen that even people who had very little in fact lived very comfortable lives. Then, all of a sudden, I came back to my country and was faced with a quite different level of poverty among school children. It grew on me gradually that you can't as a teacher say, 'OK, I'll make another sandwich for myself this time and share it.' Then you do it tomorrow and you do it the next day. But wait. The problem is bigger than you and all your sandwiches.

I had a friend who lived in a block of flats, a driving instructor and a recent convert. Playing chess was my excuse to have fellowship with him. On one occasion when I was there two or three children from the flats knocked at his door. They asked for something to eat. 'How many are you?' be asked. There were more waiting on the staircase and we asked them to come in too. He said, 'I can make you a cup of tea.' He made a big bowl of tea with just boiling water and he gave them bread that he cut in pieces. As there weren't quite enough pieces he cut them smaller, spread them with lard and fed the children. I was mesmerised. 'I do this every day,' my friend said.

A light-switch moment

Something in my mind just clicked. I thought to myself that, if he can do this, if one old man, a new Christian, can give a cup of tea and bread and lard to kids in a tiny flat in an apartment block, surely we can do more. It was then that I wrote to Blythswood explaining the problem and saying that I'd like to try to address it. 'Would you be interested in supporting the project?' I asked. The answer came quickly and the answer was yes. This happened just at the time my pastorate was coming to an end and God opened the door for me to work with Blythswood through Talita Kum.

Blythswood was also a blessing to my driving instructor friend. His name was Ardelean Ion. Ion is John. Until he died quite recently I visited him in his old people's home. I think he had always been a socially minded man but his generosity showed all the more after he became a Christian. His life changed and he was a different man. He received a filled shoebox from Blythswood each Christmas he was in the home.

So little and so much

It is almost embarrassing to see that someone with very little does something that you don't do, despite all your means and connections. I always said that the church, the community of faith, needs to do more than just preach the gospel and be happy and content with more people being added to the membership. The church needs to go out. That's something that I always argued on paper and in the pulpit. But it was this old man doing something for the children on his staircase that told me, 'It's your time; it's time for action.'

In December 2000, a good solid house built by German colonists in 1932 was purchased with Blythswood Care funds. It took us six to seven months to renovate and double it in size. We called the day-care centre 'Talita Kum' based on Jesus' words to Jairus's daughter (to which we attributed an extended metaphorical sense) because the vision then and now was to lift children up from their dire predicament. The first intake of children and official opening ceremony happened in September 2001.

In the beginning we worked with seven and eight year olds, now it is right through to fourteen-year-olds. We no longer just provide a meal and help with homework but we have a whole cultural programme with music and drama and that kind of thing. Our approach has to be holistic. Food is given on the condition that children go to school and do their homework, maintaining their education outside school hours. We found games we could play with them and creative activities they would enjoy in order that they wouldn't be playing in the street unsupervised. A Bible story has been added at the end of the day. We provide food, education, creative activities and also something to do with spiritual awareness.

Romania is not subject to secularism in the same way as much of Europe. It is more at home with its religious outlook. Romanians are suspicious of secularism because of its connections with atheism in the past. Romania's greatest challenge is perhaps nominalism, pretending or assuming that you're a Christian just because you were born in a country which has a religious outlook. Grant providers don't make a fuss about our religious outlook as long as we are not proselytising. As we are open about the content of the programme in our applications I don't feel any conflict in our use of the grants we are given.

Free ... but careful

Here in Romania we have liberties that people in the UK don't have. We're aware that the children who come within our family, within our care, are in their most formative years. They are not necessarily facing decisions about whether to be members of a church or not. Our main interest is in exposure, exposing the children to the gospel. Mostly it is at a later time in their lives that they decide to embrace Christ fully. Some have come to a decision point while they were with us, but we're not looking for decisions.

I think that what we do is try to bring the children up in the way that I was brought up as a child. It's about finding it very easy to talk about God, about Jesus, about the community of faith, about the Bible, about not being embarrassed for believing in God when others don't. What we provide is the loving, friendly and informal atmosphere that has more or less settled on the Blythswood programme here. It is not confrontational and it is encouraging. I can't think of one child who hasn't that sort of awareness of drawing to Christ in a gentle and perhaps informal way.

I admit that I have distanced myself slightly from the church. I still go to church and worship with God's people, but I am not as involved as I could be. If I'm honest, I feel reluctant to become too involved. A long time ago Paul Negrut said that he hoped that, whatever I did in life, I would not hurt the church. I think that possibility still troubles me.

Having said that I have distanced myself a little bit from the church, Talita Kum is Christian through and through. Most of my partners are Christians. The man who has been giving us bread free for years is a Christian from a Pentecostal church. We meet with him and with others like him. Some people who work with us are Christians and we have fellowship in Blythswood. I also have Christians with whom I regularly talk by email or social media, even if we sometimes disagree about theology! I maintain my spiritual temperature with the help of like-minded believers and work out my faith in action through Talita Kum.

Delphine Ndayikeza

11

'I decided to forgive' – the story of Delphine Ndayikeza and World Outreach Initiatives, Burundi

I come from a village about ninety kilometres from Bujumbura in Burundi, which is a small county and very beautiful. Burundi is densely populated, with twice the population of Scotland in a land that is about a third of the size. My father was a primary school teacher and he had cattle too. We spoke Kirundi at home and were educated in French from primary three. When we went to secondary school, aged fourteen, we began to learn English. Although I understand Swahili, I am not good at speaking the language. I am beginning by speaking about languages because some of my work today is with a radio station that broadcasts in Kirundi, French, Swahili and English. But first I will tell you my story.

When he was a boy my father had to walk many kilometres to school. He was courageous and very motivated. Dad was also motivated to send his kids to school. Many parents didn't do that even when I was young. There were seven children in our family; I am the second youngest. My earliest memory is funny. I remember how I was always asking, 'You are telling us that we were born from our parents and our parents were born from our grandparents. Now, where did those grandparents come from?' I just couldn't work it out. The answer was always 'Fore, fore, fore grandparents and they were created by God.' Then I wanted to know, 'Who created God?' They didn't have an answer and told me, 'You can't understand that. No-one can understand it.' Even as a child I wanted to know who created God. It was a very confusing question and a question without an answer.

A girl's work

My parents were Christians and we attended an Anglican church in our village. Most people in the village went to that church. I started school when I was seven but before that I helped by going out looking for water, helping with the cattle, cleaning and cooking. These were all things that a small girl did before going to school. It was a Catholic school, a good school. Protestant children went there too. At home Mum prayed with us before we went to sleep and before we went to school, also before we ate our meals.

Although I was brought up in a Christian home it was not until I was nineteen years old that I became a believer for myself. A lady came to our village, an Anglican pastor. She explained to us that not making a personal decision to become a Christian is like a student going to a school when he is not registered there. Even if he is doing great, he can't be counted amongst the students, he can't be recognised. Then she said that, if we are just going to church, worshipping with others and sharing, if we haven't made our personal decision to follow Christ, we are wasting our time. We have to have our personal inscription, our personal record. Then I realised that all these years I had wasted my time, and I decided, 'Jesus, you are my personal Saviour.'

That made a big change in my life because I was no longer just following others. Jesus was my personal friend. I read the Bible, learning what my Friend likes, what my Friend doesn't like. And I felt I had to have a personal Christian life, not just following what others were doing. Some of my friends followed Jesus, but not all of them. Quietly I watched to see how Christians lived and how they behaved and that inspired me. Carefully I watched how they did at school and their relationships with others. It was easy to do that because we were in boarding school. Only primary schools were in the villages. We had a student fellowship and found time to sit together and share about the Word of God and encourage one another. When I became a Christian I still had two more years to study at school.

To Bujumbura

Aged twenty-one, I left secondary school and went to Bujumbura to study physics. It was at university that I met Samuel, who was studying economics. He was one of the student leaders in the Christian fellowship there. In a way he was my pastor. We married, but our early years of marriage weren't easy as I had a number of miscarriages. It was very challenging. After three years at university I suspended my studies because I had to spend the whole year in South Africa for treatment. Then I came back but changed my subject to management.

After his graduation Samuel did some consultancy work for a number of months before joining a Christian organisation where he worked as a program manager. When the founder of that NGO died Samuel started on his own and that was when he founded World Outreach Initiatives. Our main objective was to contribute to rebuilding Burundi because our society had been destroyed by civil war and internal divisions. We were there to help the church to be a bridge for reconciliation and also to help the poor through a holistic Christian approach. One powerful way of doing that was to run a radio station, Radio Ivyizigiro. Many people in Burundi listen to the radio and Ivyizigiro means hope. We hold out hope to those who listen to our programmes.

Sudden tragedy

In 2002, when we had two daughters, Liana aged two and a half and one year old Elsa, Samuel was assassinated. It was so sudden. I then found myself working during the days and also doing night classes towards my management degree. That was not easy. We had met Blythswood before that and they were a great help to me. In the years since that hard time, Blythswood became not just partners but true friends. When

I took over the work after Samuel died, some people said, 'We have been working with Samuel and, as he's no longer there, we don't know what can happen with a woman's leadership…' Then they stopped communicating with me. Blythswood did not do that and it has been with their support that I've been able to go through many challenges and succeed. God has been good to me.

At that time it was really strange for a woman to be in leadership in Burundi although that has changed now. God helped me to be brave. I had to live for the future, for the future of my girls. There was no choice; I needed to carry on with the vision and the Lord has stood by me. The Word of God says that we are righteous and that we live because of faith in him. I put my trust in the Lord. Those who trust in the Lord won't be ashamed and I haven't been ashamed. Having trusted the Lord for his grace, he has been with me for his honour.

Why?

That does not mean that I was in a happy place. I was really hurt and full of very strange questions. Why Lord? Why this? Why? Why? But I can say that the Lord visited me because I was having answers inside me through the Word of God. I also had friends who came to me, encouraged me and listened and helped me to get inner healing. Then I decided, 'Lord, I don't have to think a lot about those who did it, because you allowed them to do it.' I decided to forgive and God delivered me.

Since the beginning Samuel and I were involved in healing and reconciliation and, after he died, I had to live what we had been talking about. It went beyond work, beyond theories. It became personal, practical. Now I know many widows, many people in society who are suffering because they have lost their beloved or lost their belongings. They need someone who can listen to them, who can encourage them and who can pray with them. We organised workshops where we put people together, maybe those who had the same problems. They talked about their lives, what they'd gone through, how it was affecting them and then read the Word of God and prayed together. We have seen really miraculous things happening.

Radio Ivyizigiro

There is another aspect of the radio station – our telephone line – by which we receive calls from listeners. People phone seeking advice, seeking orientation. They say, 'You know we heard about this programme on your radio. Now, if I apply that in my personal life – I'm going through this and this – what can I do to be released?' We have helpers: some counsellors, some pastors, others are people who did psychology, even doctors, and they try to help those callers. With their help we are able to provide online counselling. There is also counselling face to face though some people are not, at first, ready to come and share their problems. They start far away, calling where you can't even identify them, just asking questions. But as time goes by they can come and sit with us and then we discuss, we encourage, we pray together. Over the years we have seen a powerful impact through God blessing this ministry.

Our radio station is not involved in politics. So, when there have been political problems, we have not been affected by them. We have partnerships with different evangelical churches. Our programmes are on evangelism, health, social welfare and those kinds of things. We also broadcast youth programmes and music, but never politics. Because of that we have not had any restrictions put on us in Burundi's times of trouble.

A great support

Blythswood has been a great support to the work of World Outreach Initiatives by prayer, encouragement and just staying close. Sometimes people don't need money; they need people who can be there with them. I have benefited so much from Blythswood's care. World Outreach Initiatives run clinics that have received equipment from Blythswood. These clinics allow us to reach out to poor people and offer them good treatment at an affordable price. A great deal of stuff to help disabled people has been given to us too. Blythswood has also supported the radio station financially as the government has increased the money that we pay yearly for frequencies and pylons by almost 400 per cent. As our radio station is not profit-making, and our partners are churches who have their own financial challenges, it is difficult to afford that kind of increase in expense.

Recently we had problems in Burundi. As a Christian organisation we had to stand neutral, not supporting those who were on this side or the other, but just praying, mobilising people to be still and to stay together and stand in prayer. Our broadcasts talked about peace, about how people need to respect each other. The radio is always a good tool because, even when we can't walk in the streets, we can sit in our studio and challenge people, encourage people and pray with them. We remind listeners that the Lord is always there and he is always working for good.

Family life

I am now married to Christian. Although he is not directly involved in World Outreach Initiatives he supports us in the work. Christian is a businessman in the communications industry and he also does consultancy work. My two daughters are teenagers and at boarding school. When I was a teenager I talked with my friends because, in our culture, when you were growing up your parents didn't talk to you. They thought you would learn everything you needed to know at school. I am able to talk to my daughters about life, about challenges they might meet, how they can even meet bad friends, how they have to make their own decisions. I try to encourage them to have their own vision and to avoid anything or anyone trying to stop them from achieving their goals. Christian and I have three young children. Caleb is nine, Graddy is seven and Keyla is six. They are all at school now because today children in cities start when they are three.

Life is very different for our children from my life when I was a village girl. We had to work so much, helping our parents in many ways. Now we live in the city and have a house-girl and a house-boy helping in our home. That does not mean that our children are not as busy as we were, but they are not working as we worked. We do not allow them television or distractions like that. Christian and I spend a great deal of time with the children. They cannot run outside and play as we did in the village. And, while they are interested in the animals when we go back to visit, they cannot milk a cow as I could at their ages.

The value of a cow

Wealth in rural places means having a lot of cows because, when you have cows, you have fertiliser and you can increase your harvest. You also have milk. But, if you are among the rural poor, life is still very miserable. There are households of orphans in our villages and widows who are in desperate need of help and encouragement. Through World Outreach Initiatives we support those families to enable them to improve their income. We encourage children to go to school, and those who have grown up can attend schools to learn technical skills which can enable them to start small businesses and take up other income generating activities.

There are still children in Burundi who are not able to read and write, especially boys and girls and young people living on the streets. They are usually there because they have lost their parents. The poorest children still can't go to school. Although the government says that education is free of charge, going to school means more than school fees. They have to buy the uniform; they have to buy food. If the choice is going to school or eating, a child will always eat. You can see that there are still many needs in Burundi, still so much work for us to do.

Helping hands

I will tell you about some of the ways we are able to help. We supply some of those who are poor with well selected seeds and goats or chickens or pigs. Then people can earn money to send their children to school while getting food and fertilisers from their cattle as well. We're also involved in community work in our clinics. More than 1,000 people living with HIV are helped through them. World Outreach Initiatives provide them with free counselling and tests and support pregnant women, assisting them all the way through and helping the newborn, trying to make sure that the baby is not contaminated. We see HIV negative babies born in HIV positive families. While mothers almost always feed their babies for six months, some poor families need food assistance because mothers can't breast-feed. These children are given assistance until they are about eighteen months old and they need very close follow up.

World Outreach Initiatives helps start income generating activities. One lady sells onions, buying five kilograms of onions and selling them to her neighbours one by one. Others sell charcoal, or small fish from the lake, or make and sell soap. There's one man who buys a crate of Fanta and sells the cans individually at a profit. Some girls want to sew, but don't have machines yet. We organise training for these people and then put them in small associations, self-help groups where each member is accountable to the others. And we also encourage volunteers to become community health workers. They teach family health and hygiene, do HIV tests and other comparatively simple, but effective, work. Another very important part of their work is teaching about the use of mosquito nets, the only way that malaria can be controlled. Community health workers are dedicated. They do a great job and none of them are paid.

Vital listeners

Of course community health workers help Christians and people of no faith or of another faith. That is also true of Radio Ivyizigiro. A survey done by a French company showed that we are the fifth most popular radio station in Burundi. It also showed that most of our listeners are women and children. They are vital listeners. If women hear our message, they will pass it on to the next generation. And hearing about peace and reconciliation could change the course of a young listener's life.

We receive testimonies from different people who have problems, who were at the point of suicide, and who changed their minds because of our broadcasts. It's not evangelism; it's not making noise. It's just talking to people, teaching how they can face their challenges. And we hear of people who changed their beliefs, of Muslims being saved. Our programmes are not only for church people because, if we're dealing with wounds, we address everyone for each one of us has our own wounds. So many Burundians are living with loss. We encourage people to sit together, talk about their past and try to cope with it and face the future. When we organise a workshop or talk on the radio, it's not for a targeted group, it's for all listeners. Our coverage stretches throughout Burundi, part of Rwanda, Congo and a small part of Tanzania. We have great opportunities and great challenges.

A complete turnaround

I remember when one young woman heard people saying that Jesus would come back, she was very happy. In the workshop she opened up and said, 'You know, I'm happy Jesus will come back and punish my mum.' She had such deep hurts that she couldn't even face her mother. It was a terrible situation. After the workshop, after talking, she was able to sit with her mum. They talked and asked for forgiveness. Then they were reconciled and the daughter died peacefully a few months later.

We have some challenges that face us just now. Clinic facilities need renewing, especially the clinics in slum areas, because they have been there since 2001 and their capacity is limited. The ambulance Blythswood gave us helps in our work and also sometimes brings income because others can rent it from us if they need to transfer patients to Rwanda, where there is a good health service. That ambulance is one of the best in Burundi. While we really thank Blythswood and others for supporting us, we need to have our own ways of generating income to help sustain our programmes. It can happen that donors get tired, or have economic crises, and are no longer able to give aid even when the need for it remains. God is good and has provided for all that has been done so far. He will not fail us.

Balazs Csiszer

12

I went at night – the story of Balazs Csiszer, Bonus Pastor Foundation and the Daniel Centre, Romania

I was brought up in Romania, in an ethnic Hungarian family. We were atheists. Dad was a Party member because he had to be, but he wasn't communist in his thinking. Maybe he was in his early days, but by the 1980s he was very much against the Party and what it represented in Romania. My mother's father passed away and she was raised by her mother and her grandparents. Her grandparents were convinced Adventists. From the moment she left home Mum had no religion at all.

Today Mum respects me and what I believe, but still seems sure it is not for her. The only time I ever heard about God in my family was in the context of the dark ages when people could be fooled into believing anything. My first time in a church was when I was fifteen and went to see my cousin professing faith in front of a congregation. We were late and had to sit in the front row. I was growing fast and my jacket was too short. The lasting memory is of complete embarrassment.

In high school we had a philosophy class when I was sixteen; that was in 1987. I remember one of the girls asking the teacher what he believed, what denomination he belonged to and what church he attended. He looked very surprised and asked, 'We're all Marxists, aren't we?' Then some of the girls said that they weren't Marxists, that they were Christians. I was really surprised. They were such nice people that I couldn't understand how they could be Christians. That started arguments and debates in the classroom. Soon afterwards I heard that the girls had become Christians through attending a Bible study group run by Levente Horvath. I didn't know it then, but Levente would become one of my best friends.

Wrong type

Very soon after that I started dating one of these girls and her biggest problem was Levente's wife Maria, who told her that she shouldn't go out with a non-Christian. That made me think Christians weren't interested in me because I was the wrong type of person. About then a friend became a Christian through Levente's Bible study group. He and I argued a lot about religion. Eventually my friend arranged for me to visit Levente. I chose to go at night in order that people wouldn't see me.

Maria wasn't at home and Levente was looking after their child. He and I talked for three hours. I was quite impressed, not necessarily with Christianity at that point, but with Levente. His basic message was that not all Christians are idiots.

My curiosity was raised. He was wise and didn't invite me to join the Bible study group with the other teenagers. Instead he asked me to meet with an older group. I went along a good number of times and then he was moved away from Targu Mures and the meetings stopped.

I met many interesting people through Levente and began to realise that Christians weren't old fashioned and didn't live in another world. Eventually I reached a stage where I thought Christianity made sense and decided that faith really worked for believers, but I couldn't believe. What I needed was proof to make sense of it all. That was towards the end of high school when I was eighteen years old.

No free choice

There was a system for those of us who wanted to go to university and it was quite difficult to be accepted. My parents had sent me to a school which focussed on mathematics and physics though in those days nobody ever asked what you wanted to become when you grew up. The best students from my school went on to become maths and physics teachers. But I wasn't one of the outstanding students and I was told that I should become a construction engineer or a mechanical engineer. At that time we were informed by our schools what we were to do; we did not have a free choice.

I took the exam to study mechanical engineering and was selected. The stakes were quite high to get into a university with military service because, if you did, you only served nine months before becoming an officer, well not quite an officer. What happened was that, in the case of mobilisation, you would immediately be advanced to lieutenant. Our rank would be sub lieutenant. If you didn't make it to university, military service was two months training and then hard labour for another sixteen months. So it mattered quite a lot.

Him or me

That's how I came to be in the army in Brasov in December 1989 when the revolution happened. I was eighteen years old and found myself caught in a gun fight with one of the guns in my hand. This is what happened. We were handed live ammunition and our lieutenant, who was twenty-three, gathered us for a briefing. 'If ordered, you have to shoot,' we were told. 'It's better that his or her mother cries rather than your mother.' He turned to me and said, 'Do you understand, Csiszer?' I heard myself say that I didn't think I could shoot innocent people. 'Right Csiszer,' barked the lieutenant, 'you stay right next to me all the time and I will personally watch you.' My colleagues, who were eighteen-year-olds like me, all felt the same as I did. 'Lieutenant,' said one, 'I will have to stand right next to Csiszer because I feel the same.' And then other voices joined in, saying, 'Me too,' 'And me too,' and 'Me too.' It was really intense. Thanks to God's goodness (though I didn't know that then) we were not ordered to go out against the demonstrators.

The following night, when the shooting really started in Brasov against the so-called terrorists, we were marched out into action. It was chaos. It was the kind of total chaos that took us over. It didn't cross my mind whether God existed or not when I fired my weapon. We wanted to shoot at the vehicles coming towards us. To be totally honest, I didn't feel bad. I just fired.

We were due to finish military service at the end of June but, because of all the changes that followed the revolution, the authorities decided not to complete our training and released us. After a six month break, it was time for my first classes in Cluj. That summer, through the influence of my girlfriend, I went to a Christian camp. It was run by Americans and I went because I'd studied English but had never had an opportunity to use the language. I thought it would be good to try it out. I really liked the community feeling, the songs and the whole atmosphere of the camp but I didn't become a Christian. Then when college started, I began to attend a students' Bible study group and that's where I met Levente again. He was in Cluj by then.

Something still missing

The following summer, that was 1991, I attended the same camp and that was the first time I prayed to God saying I wanted to become a Christian and asking him to reveal himself to me. I don't know what I expected to happen, but it felt as if nothing changed. Later the Americans told me that, when they went home, in the American way they had to give a report back to their congregation about how many had been converted and I was the only one. It wasn't a very big success story for their church.

Although I felt the same as before, some things did change. One was that I became really hungry to learn and I started to read books about the Christian faith, whether or not it made sense, whether or not it could be proved. About two months later, on my knees, I invited Christ into my heart. That was the point when I said, 'OK, I'm a Christian.' But something was still missing, really missing. My faith felt like a one-way thing. I had high expectations of myself in terms of how my behaviour would change, hoping that my wrong desires would all go away. They didn't.

At that time I didn't feel that my sins were forgiven. It didn't click even though I was trying really hard. I called myself a Christian and struggled to live up to the standards I thought were demanded of me. That was for about a year and a half. I didn't take part in Communion despite going to church. One Sunday I was sitting in the upper floor of the church watching everyone taking Communion and I've never felt so lonely in my life. I'd had lonely moments before, and even do today, but I've never again felt how I felt that day. I decided it was simple. I'd be baptised and confirmed. Then I'd take Communion and my temptations would stop.

The crucial question

I decided to speak to a mature Christian and we talked and talked. I told him about my problems, temptations and sins. After some time he said, 'It's ok. Stop now. Do you believe that Christ died for your sins?' He stopped me focussing on my temptations and on my sins and made me focus on Christ.

After that I was baptised and had to give my testimony. I didn't elaborate on my sins and shortcomings. But later that night I still felt frustrated. I still didn't feel different. On the way home, as I thought things through, something clicked and I suddenly realised that no matter how hard we try, we don't qualify. That was the first time I felt what the forgiveness of sins is. And that was the moment from which I call myself a Christian. I knew then what relief was and peace. It had taken me about three years to reach that stage. It was a long time.

When I first told my mother I was a believer and really serious about my faith, she started to cry, saying that they'd got me, they'd fooled me. Gradually she accepted that I had changed. With my father it was a big battle. We had a very bad relationship. He was quite an aggressive man, not someone to get close to. That caused me a problem because the Bible told me to respect my parents and taught that Christians need to forgive the hurts others have caused them. When the 'other' is your father, that is difficult.

Parent problems

I tried to take this problem seriously and sat down with Dad to talk but we always ended up in a big argument. Each time I started off saying I wanted to respect him but ended up shouting, telling him what an awful person he was and how he would die lonely and miserable. It was just a total and complete disaster and failure. I didn't tell Dad I was going to be baptised but phoned him afterwards with the news. He just said, 'OK.' But the following week he took my younger and older sisters with him to a Reformed Church and they were all accepted and baptised! I don't know why the church accepted them because neither of my sisters was a believer at that stage. Dad's excuse was that you had to belong somewhere.

Later that year there was a day when Dad and I sat down and had a good talk, the first one that didn't end in disaster. It was when my older sister decided to move to Hungary which, in those days, was considered almost like treason. My father was very disappointed. I explained to him why I didn't want to leave. It wasn't a question of whether I'm Hungarian or Romanian; that's irrelevant to me. The question was, 'Where does God want me and what is his plan for my life?' I told Dad that I had no desire to leave but, if God guided in that direction, I would go. He looked at me and said, 'You know what? You may be right.' We parted in peace and I went back to Cluj. Later that same day Mum phoned to say Dad had suffered a third massive heart attack and died. That was the only time after I became a believer that we discussed Christianity or mentioned God without it ending up in an argument.

The lonely years

There was a long time between me becoming a Christian and being married. That was a lonely time although it was a learning time for me as a Christian. Then in 2005 I met Agnes. Over my lonely years I think I learned about relationships and about sharing. I'd say that's partly why we're in a happy marriage. Before that I would have been too shy to say some things. And I'd have been afraid to share my fears because, as a man, you don't face your fears or even admit they exist. What I learned over that long time helps our marriage and helps me in my work too. I think my experiences made me more mature in the way I deal with human issues.

That is the story of me learning about my emotions. Now I will tell you about my work starting as graduation came close. I was desperately praying to God about what he wanted me to do but he didn't seem to answer. At one point, I think probably six months before graduation, Levente approached me with an idea, as he quite often does. My friend asked if I wanted to help him set up Bonus Pastor Foundation, a ministry reaching out to alcoholics.

The job would be to manage the construction of a therapy centre but, of course, he had no money. I had someone in my family who was an alcoholic and that put me off this kind of work. I said, 'No, you know what alcoholics are like. And I'm not a builder, I'm a mechanical engineer.' When I grew more desperate, I thought, 'Why not?' So I asked God if he wanted me to be involved and, if he did, would he make Levente ask me again. One week before my final exam, he asked me again. I agreed to do it for the summer. I think I had my last exam on a Friday and my first work session with Levente the following Monday.

Bonus Pastor

A few days later Levente had a camp starting at a Christian campsite. A hundred people were going. At least half were alcoholics and the others were relatives who were going with them. Of course the job wasn't managing construction, it was organising the camp. The first night a group of people arrived by train. I was supposed to meet them at the station and then the following morning we'd all go by bus up the mountain to the very remote camp with no electricity. I met the train and this guy rolled off into my arms and asked who I was. I told him I was Balazs and he said that he thought we were going to get on fine and understand each other very well. To be honest, I took that as coming from God. Of course, the guy not only smelled of alcohol but also of homelessness, of street life. And that was just the beginning.

Those twelve days of camp are among the best memories I have. Levente's sermons were a real blessing. And it was amazing just being with these guys and watching them: first day shaking, second day shaking, gradually their faces changing and the feeling of community growing all the time. We had one very intense day when a guy disappeared. He had signs of delirium tremens and thought that everyone else in the room had devil's horns. Locking the others in the house with a big wooden bar, he disappeared into the hills in his pyjamas and without even slippers on his feet.

It would take too long to tell, but that whole story was a close encounter with God. At the end of the twelve days at camp I thought this was really exciting work. That autumn I agreed with Levente that I would continue with Bonus Pastor for another six months. We totally forgot to renew our agreement and six months became ten years. The ethos of Bonus

Pastor is: don't tell me these things because you think I'd like to hear them. I could work with that, and did for that long time.

The Daniel Centre

In 2002 things changed when I started working part-time with Blythswood while continuing to work with Bonus Pastor. Now I am employed full-time by Blythswood as their Chief Executive in Romania and much of my work is with the Daniel Centre. This is a transit home that can accommodate up to eighteen young men who have grown up in state care. They come to us at the age of eighteen for help with basic life skills, emotional support, and training in the ethics of work. Through our partner organisations they gain work skills which equip them for full-time employment or further education. Community is so important in the Christian life. In a modified therapeutic community such as the Daniel Centre there is positive peer pressure as we mirror each other in love. The purpose is to lift each other.

One thing which is important in my work is remembering what God has taught me through my life's experiences. He has made me aware of my shortcomings and my problems and that helps me to understand what's happening in others. For example, what are realistic expectations? What does God really expect from us? I'm there just to ensure that we're within the set structure but it's really what the boys share, and how they support each other, that's important.

God wants us to be open and honest about problems and to allow other people to be the same. I think that gives a freedom, especially for a group of boys such as we have in the Daniel Centre, boys who are here to talk about problems. They want and need to talk about sensitive issues and, if there is somebody who is quite relaxed about opening a sensitive subject, that helps. If you are relaxed enough to raise an issue, and be gentle and loving to individuals rather than only giving moral dos and don'ts, it's liberating for the whole group. That's my experience.

Life at the Centre

Because the Daniel Centre is now a licensed social service provider, technically it can be a successful programme even if we don't mention anything Christian. But our success is in opening up the perspective of the gospel to our clients. Quite a number of our guys attend church regularly and some of them, probably most of them, would say they are believers. I think many are. A few know the Bible better than I do! We don't force the subject, rather we try to open it up as issues arise. We can't take our boys to church if they don't want to come. But on Sundays there is a two or three hour period when we close the Centre. If the guys want to walk in the park, that's fine. A good number choose to come to church. We have a Bible study group which is not compulsory but they all attend. And we have prayer before our meals.

My years working at the Daniel Centre have brought great joy and a sense of achievement. Since it opened sixteen years ago, around one-hundred young men have benefited. Of course, there have been disappointments and failures but even in these cases there will have been some positive effect on young lives. Our faith has been tested daily. We persevere in what we do and believe but we need to learn to let people go. Ultimately it's between God and the individual. When the time is right for change or transformation, it happens.

It's challenging to work with people who have been disadvantaged in their background and may be below average in their mental or emotional abilities. We are confronted by how narrow-minded and hypocritical we can be in what we expect in terms of change or development. What seems nothing to me might be a big success to one of the Daniel Centre boys. Being part of this work is an exciting adventure.

Finlay Mackenzie

13

Challenge Finlay – the story of Finlay Mackenzie and Blythswood Care in Eastern Europe

I was brought up in the north of Scotland in a Free Church of Scotland family. We went to church twice a week, every week, and we were taught to understand the Bible. While all that was true, neither parents or children were believers. At that time we would have been called good church people, but that didn't make us Christians. The Free Church of Scotland took teaching children very seriously; there were even annual exams in Scripture knowledge when I was young. I took part in them until my mid teens. My parents encouraged me to do that. It's a strange thing to say, but I had quite a Christian upbringing, even though my parents were not then converted.

In my youth Communion lasted over a whole weekend in the Free Church and it still does in some places. I remember one Fast Day morning (the Fast Day was the Thursday of the

Communion weekend), going from home downhill to church in Strathpeffer with my grandad. I was thinking that I could be doing something more interesting than going to church. Grandad slid in the mud and fell. He wasn't hurt but he was so covered in mud that there was nothing for it but to turn and climb all the way back home. I was as happy as he was not. God still had a lot of work to do in me!

As a boy my one ambition was to drive a snow plough. Where we lived we used to see them clearing the snow every winter. That ambition was realised when I worked as a road-man for Highland Council for ten years. Of course, winter was my favourite time of year for that's when I climbed on to the snow plough and headed out in the worst of weathers to do, what I thought, was the best of jobs.

A real turnaround

My father was a crofter and he worked the land, often with me giving him a hand. We worked well together but, as his health broke, he began asking me what was to be done rather than telling me what to do. That was a real turnaround! When I arrived one day in 1985 to help Dad on the croft, Mum said, 'Your father has professed faith.' In my denomination that expression meant that Dad had been converted and had spoken to the Kirk Session (the church leadership) and had been accepted for membership. I remember just walking down the field and really not knowing what to think. Strangely, I'd always thought that Mum would profess faith before Dad. There was a real change in Dad after that.

By then I was married to Wendy and had drifted a bit from church, going once a month rather than twice a week to the local Free Church in Dingwall. Our minister moved to another congregation and Rev John Angus Macleod came in his place. I remember going home from his induction praying that God would not leave me behind. I can't explain that but the Holy Spirit must have been working in my heart for I went back to my old practice of attending twice every Sunday. I can honestly say that I enjoyed the preaching, the singing, the whole church experience.

Momentous changes

In December 1989 Dad died. That was a hard time but the church people were so kind to the family. In fact, their love made me start to think more about Christ and more about salvation. While losing Dad was a momentous thing in my life, momentous things were also happening elsewhere in the world that same month, and I couldn't but be aware of them thanks to the television news. Communism was falling and revolutions were in the headlines. The revolution in Romania made a profound impact across the world due to the pictures of orphans that shocked everyone who saw them. I had no idea then how much of an influence that was going to have on my life.

Some time before Dad died I had come to the conclusion that Christianity was for other folk, just not for me. But I couldn't get away from it that easily. I remember starting to go to the first of the weekend services, despite having decided not to. While I don't remember what the minister preached on,

I do remember him shutting his Bible. Then he turned round as if looking at the blank wall behind him and said, 'You have to remember that Christ died for you.' As he quoted some verses of Isaiah 53 I knew that I needed to be right with God, that I needed to follow Jesus. I professed faith the next night. That was in September 1990 and my whole world changed. I knew that my prayer was answered, that I'd not been left behind.

Wendy wasn't with me at church. In fact, she just attended from time to time. And she was so uncomfortable with ministers that when one came to visit, she would go out the back door as he came in the front. I explained to Wendy that I couldn't do anything else but believe that Jesus was my Saviour and I prayed that she would also come to know him. There was a complete change of life. I started going to prayer meetings and became interested in many different Christian things. Looking back on it now, I realise that was a very good time.

God's call

Three months later, on a frosty December evening, I came home from gritting the road. It was a Saturday evening and the television was on. We worked long hours and I needed to unwind before going to bed. So I sat down to watch a programme called 'Challenge Anneke'. Anneke Rice gave people different challenges, or people came to her telling her what they'd like to do. That night it showed a convoy of aid trucks going to Romania and also a group of men helping to repair an orphanage. I couldn't believe what I was seeing. By the time the programme was finished the television picture was blurred by tears. I asked the Lord then if he would allow me to go. I had no desire to be on television, nothing like that, but I knew I had to help some way or another if I possibly could.

Not long after that I was at the church prayer meeting and one of the ladies told me that Blythswood had been in town collecting clothing and other things for Eastern Europe. I asked what she meant and she explained that Blythswood was going to transport aid to Romania. 'I'd love to do that,' I said. The woman advised me to speak to Jackie Ross. Jackie was so involved in so many things that catching him wasn't the easiest thing in the world to do. About six months went past with me wondering whether or not this was for me. I continued to pray that I would be able to go.

At that time a young man started coming to church and we often asked him for a coffee afterwards. 'Not tonight,' was his frequent reply, but one night he did come. When we got speaking he told me he had just started working with Blythswood, helping Jackie Ross to organise all the different things he was involved in. 'I would love to do that,' I told him. 'Well,' said he, 'we'll have to get you sorted out. But we've a problem this week. We need to get a van to Glasgow and a lorry to Aberdeen at the end of the week. Do you know anybody who could help?' 'Yes, I do,' I told him, 'I have three days holiday at the end of this week. I'll do it.'

Blythswood

That was my first introduction to Blythswood and it was in September 1991. I took Jackie's car round half a dozen churches collecting food and other things. Then I helped to pack it in boxes because I had to take it to Glasgow the next day for three men from Lewis who were about to leave with a load for Albania. I phoned Wendy and asked her to come down and help us to pack the boxes and the two of us have been there ever since, in a manner of speaking!

That Friday I took the lorry to Aberdeen and went back for it on the following Saturday. From then on I did what I could for Blythswood. As I had trained as a tractor mechanic on leaving school, I was able to refurbish tractors that were transported out to Eastern Europe. Eventually, in 1992 I had the opportunity to go not only to Romania but also to Albania with another driver, Keith Martin. For somebody from my background in highland Scotland that experience was just mind-blowing.

Push!

We arrived late on a Saturday night in Romania. While I felt so thankful that the Lord let me go, I was still asking myself what in the world I was doing there! Entering the country was beyond chaotic. I couldn't get over how people waiting in the queue at the border pushed their cars forward to save fuel rather than starting the engine to drive just one stage forward in the queue. The border guards were drunk. There was a little hut from which a hand came out – that was the Hungarian hand that took our papers and then disappeared. From there we walked round to the other side of the hut and eventually a Romanian hand came out and handed our papers back again.

The typewriter the hand used was so stiff that every key had to be pressed down twice.

The first building I entered in Romania was a prison. On the Sunday morning we were taken there by a missionary from Northern Ireland who had been a terrorist in the troubles there. Six or seven, sometimes even eight, men were in each small cell. They were almost like bread trays packed on racks. That afternoon we went to visit a church in Marghita which, although I didn't realise it at the time, would become one of the churches that I would work with long-term and right to the present day.

Answered prayer

Keith and I had an amazing experience in Timisoara, in central Romania, on the way to Albania. We couldn't get under a bridge. It was late at night and we turned around and tried another street, but couldn't get under the bridge there either. We decided that the best thing to do was to pray. Both of us prayed and, just as Keith finished praying, a car drew up. The driver wound down his window and, in perfect English, asked if we were lost. We explained our problem and told him where we were going. 'Follow me,' he said, and that's what we did, all round the city and out the other side. Keith suggested we should give him something a small thank you gift. I went into the cab for some chocolate while Keith was having a look underneath the lorry. When we turned round the man wasn't there. Both man and car had disappeared. We could see for far enough but we couldn't see any tail lights. I believe that was my first experience of a messenger being sent from the Lord to help us.

From Romania, Keith and I drove through Yugoslavia and then down to Albania with our second lorry-load of aid. If Romania was different from anywhere I'd been before, Albania was completely different. The country hadn't been open for very long. In fact, the van I helped to load the previous September was the first Blythswood vehicle to go to Albania and I think our one was the fourth. As we drove south of Belgrade we noticed that there was no traffic coming up the motorway on the other side. Then, when we came round a big bend, we could see lots of tanks and military vehicles coming up towards us. It was the start of the Balkan wars, the Bosnian war.

Albania

Nothing prepared us for going in to Albania. We were about twelve hours at the border because we had to take everything off the truck that was removable. From there we set off for Tirana. If a policeman tried to stop us, we just went round him. Had we stopped we could have been mugged or robbed. And there was no point in asking the police for help as they'd no means of finding information, no phones, nothing. Of course, that meant that, if we didn't stop for one policeman, he had no way of letting the next one along the road know that we were coming!

I remember driving uphill towards Tirana. It took about two and a half hours to go up and then down the other side.

There was absolute silence, no cars, no buses, no trucks, nothing moving at all until the next morning. And the minister of health himself came to help unload the truck because we had medical stuff with us. The hospital in Tirana had nothing, not even windows. I had never seen a hospital without windows. It was so dark inside that they had people who walked around with their hand on our shoulders to make sure we got to where we were going.

Wendy was with me on nearly all my road trips to Eastern Europe but she wasn't on the first one as she had become a Christian and was professing her faith while we were away. Apart from that time these trips have been done together. As I was still working as a roadman we went twice a year, in spring and autumn. So we've both had the privilege of meeting Christians in Eastern Europe and hearing about their lives, about what they've suffered. The people we've met have made a huge impression on us. In fact, they've changed our lives.

A big decision

Several times Jackie Ross asked me to consider working for Blythswood full-time. Wendy and I prayed about it but it just didn't feel right. Then he asked again in 1995. The winter programme had already been made up and I didn't want to leave my work until March. So, after one last winter on the snow plough, I left work as a roadman and started with Blythswood.

Jackie, who was one of the founders of Blythswood, was a driven man, driven by the love for Christ and love for people. He was not perfect and nearly drove folk to distraction from time to time with all his ideas and all that he wanted to do. But he was great to work with. I think he was a very humble and shy man in many ways. He took incredible risks but it's my opinion that he took risks because God led him. If you were willing to get on and do things, he would do everything to help you. But I don't think he was too keen on people who weren't willing to put their all into what they were doing. When I went to work with Jackie my remit was to look after the transport and all the vehicles. That's not the only door that God has opened for me to go through. He also led me into becoming a lay preacher in pulpits at home and in Eastern Europe. He certainly is the God of surprises!

No Brownie points

On the humanitarian side, I think the contribution to the work of Blythswood of people who are not Christians has been invaluable. It never ceases to amaze me how committed to the work some of them are. To my mind it's one thing to decide to do something for others, but it's a completely different thing to do it knowing that Christ is with you. I think some of these volunteers have been greatly affected by the people they've met. It is so clear to see that Eastern European believers live their faith as well as believe it when you hear what they've gone through.

Of course, many of the people – probably most of the people – who contribute to Blythswood are not Christians. And it concerns me that some of those who donate things, or who help in other ways, feel they are somehow earning

God's praise. I've heard folk say, 'Well, I'm OK now. That's me earned a few more Brownie points.' Comments like that make me sad and concerned. The truth is that none of us can earn our way to heaven. Jesus is the Way, the Truth and the Life and there is no other way to heaven than to believe on him and rely on the grace of God.

Partners

Many of the projects that we're involved in today have grown from relationships made in our early days of delivering aid. From the initial loads in trucks grew involvement in communities. Christians asked if we could help them, often with specific projects, and we've done that where we've been able. Nowadays my role is to encourage our brothers and sisters here in the UK, to encourage our partners in Eastern Europe and elsewhere, and to look at how we do things and at how they might be done differently. Blythswood works in partnership with others and the partnerships are equal. Blythswood is a founding member of Global Hand, an umbrella organisation set up in 2002 to share resources between organisations. I am one of the trustees.

One part of scripture I find very encouraging is Revelation chapters seven and twenty-one where John sees the masses of people gathered together before God's throne in heaven and asks who they are and where they come from. It's amazing to think that each and every one of us who belong to Christ is there, that we are part of that great number. And it is wonderful to be assured that in heaven we won't hunger or thirst any more. But I think the most beautiful part of that section is that there will be no more tears. We live in a world of tears and sometimes we may have seen too many tears. During the early days in Romania, in the children's homes, there were terrible sights and many broken-hearted tears. In heaven there will be no more tears and all God's people will be able to worship him together joyfully.

Looking back

Blythswood was not the first to go from Easter Ross to Eastern Europe. Elizabeth Ross, whose father was the banker in Tain, began her medical training just two years after women were first allowed to study medicine. Following several years working as a doctor on a Scottish island, in Persia and as a ship's surgeon, she learned of the urgent need in Serbia at the beginning of World War 1. Most of the country's 400 doctors were in war service. Elizabeth was one of several Scottish women to answer that call. Sadly a typhus epidemic ravaged the country killing tens of thousands, Dr Ross among them. She survived less than three weeks in Serbia and died on 14th February, 1915. Today she is remembered nationally each year on the anniversary of her death. Her name is a byword for courage and self-sacrifice and her story is still told in Serbian schools.

Rolling forward seventy-five years takes us to the first Blythswood lorries heading from Easter Ross to Eastern Europe. The countries we work in are very different now compared to how they were then. Even in my time I've seen great changes. Eastern Europe is more prosperous and more materialistic; it is no less religious but it is less Christian. There seems to me to be less of a hunger for the gospel and more of a hunger for possessions.

Of course, each of the countries that make up Eastern Europe was different; all were emerging from Communism but each had its own history. For example, in Romania some churches were built during communist times while in Albania that was inconceivable. Modern Albanian Christian history just dates back to 1992. Albania was the most closed country. The country was peppered with concrete pillbox shelters by way of protection against a perceived American threat. Albanians were told that theirs was the most affluent country in the world and that the Americans couldn't wait to take it over. The land has gone from being closed and unspeakably poor to one of the most advanced in Eastern Europe over the fifteen years between my first and last visits. And the hill outside Tirana that took us two and a half hours to drive up? It has been replaced by a tunnel and the journey now takes forty-five minutes!

The other countries in which we work have undergone their own changes. Romania is now a modern society with an emerging middle class. The IT industry is big and growing and fields that have never been ploughed in all my years of visiting are now growing crops. But I don't detect such a hunger for the gospel these days. There seems to me to be more of a spiritual hunger in Moldova. It too has changed but in some ways it's a divided country with young people looking west to Europe and older people looking east to Russia.

Bananas

Serbia is a land of contrasts with the central southern area being the least evangelised part of Europe. After I preached in a church recently there a young woman told me that she had introduced her family to the Bible just the previous week. They had never seen one before. Serbians seem to be more welcoming that most to the current wave of migrants crossing Europe. Perhaps they are remembering their own history.

Which brings me to bananas. Because so many different cultural and religious groups are represented in the great 21st Century migrant movement, there can be real problems in providing food aid. One food that every religious group will eat is bananas and they give an energy surge that is amazing to see. Blythswood has taken between eleven and twelve tons of bananas over recent months to the migrant camp near the Serbian Macedonian border.

That's not the only crisis we've tried to meet. We were already working on Kosovo when their troubles broke out and we did what we could to help. Hungary is very western in many ways, yet less than an hour from the capital there is desperate poverty. And Bulgaria continues to be the poorest country in the European Union. Our work there is limited to delivering Christmas shoeboxes and that is also our continuing ministry to Kosovo.

FIRE!

While Blythswood started fifty years ago providing emergency aid it has, in many places, developed into an organisation that gives long-term support. For the last fifteen years our 999 Project has done both. There are few more urgent needs than a fire that is out of control. But not all Eastern European countries have the infrastructure which we are used to. That's why our 999 project came into being. Retired fire engines have been acquired, refurbished and sent out to where they were most needed. There are twelve in Moldova, six in Romania and fifteen in Serbia. Those who operate them have been trained in their use and in the response to road traffic accidents. We have also sent ambulances to Moldova, Serbia and Burundi. So urgent needs are met and provision made for the long term.

Basically Blythswood does the same now as it did fifty years ago. It's a Christian investment agency, with the investment being in people, in churches, in communities and in countries. Some of the investment is in terms of finance, some in teaching, some in aid, some in services, and some in support. But without the investment in prayer it would all come to nothing, and that's an investment in which every reader of this book can be a part.

Last word

It is nearly twenty-five years since I first volunteered with Blythswood, and they are twenty-five years I would never have missed. The years have brought blessings and challenges, and most of all they've brought the joy of knowing that we are making a difference, that we are meeting people at the point of their need and helping. Blythswood is part of history, part of HIS STORY, part of God's plan. At the end of the 20th Century God brought about huge changes in one sixth of the world when Communism fell and closed countries opened up. Blythswood has been part of the response to that change and I thank God that I have been part of it too. God is so good.

Blythswood Care and you

If you have been challenged by the testimonies in
this book and would like further help with
Bible study please email

biblecourse@blythswood.org

or write to
**Blythswood Care, Highland Deephaven,
Evanton IV16 9XJ**

You can support the ministry of Blythswood Care by
praying, by giving, by forming a support group
or by volunteering.

For more information on the work of
Blythswood Care, go to www.blythswood.org

Blythswood's annual Shoe Box Appeal
can be found at www.shoeboxappeal.org

Blythswood Care
Highland Deephaven
Evanton
IV16 9XJ

Tel. 01349 830777

Scottish charity number SC021848

Christian Focus Publications

Our mission statement –

STAYING FAITHFUL

In dependence upon God we seek to impact the world through literature faithful to His infallible Word, the Bible. Our aim is to ensure that the Lord Jesus Christ is presented as the only hope to obtain forgiveness of sin, live a useful life and look forward to heaven with Him.

Our books are published in four imprints:

CHRISTIAN
FOCUS

Popular works including biographies, commentaries, basic doctrine and Christian living.

CHRISTIAN
HERITAGE

Books representing some of the best material from the rich heritage of the church.

MENTOR

Books written at a level suitable for Bible College and seminary students, pastors, and other serious readers. The imprint includes commentaries, doctrinal studies, examination of current issues and church history.

CF4•K

Children's books for quality Bible teaching and for all age groups: Sunday school curriculum, puzzle and activity books; personal and family devotional titles, biographies and inspirational stories – because you are never too young to know Jesus!

Christian Focus Publications Ltd,
Geanies House, Fearn, Ross-shire,
IV20 1TW, Scotland, United Kingdom.
www.christianfocus.com